UNDERSTANDING YOUR HIGH FUNCTIONING AUTISTIC CHILD

A PARENT'S GUIDE TO NAVIGATING THE NEW
DIAGNOSIS, WITH STRATEGIES TO HELP YOU
AND YOUR CHILD THRIVE.

MAUREEN M. WILKINSON

Section Publishing

licensed professional before attempting any techniques outlined in this book.

By reading this document, the reader agrees that under no circumstances is the author responsible for any losses, direct or indirect, which are incurred as a result of the use of the information contained within this document, including, but not limited to, — errors, omissions, or inaccuracies.

A SPECIAL GIFT TO ALL OUR READERS!

Included with the purchase of this book is '7 Life-changing Tools to Get Your Child To Sleep.' The guide will provide you with fundamental strategies to get your child's bedtime routine on track and help them sleep through the night!

Visit the website below and let us know which email address to send it to:

maureen@maureenmwilkinson.com

CONTENTS

INTRODUCTION

You have recently learned that your child has High Functioning Autism (HFA). You are confused and do not know what to do. There are an astronomical amount of tips and guides on the web, which can often be overwhelming, and it is more than likely you do not know where or how to start. You want to give the best to your HFA child, but at the same time, you feel lost. You may be feeling guilty about all of these things, but let me tell you one important thing: I was just like you at the start of this journey. To show you that you are not alone, allow me to begin this book with a personal story.

When my son, who is high-functioning, was 7, he got invited to his cousin's birthday party. We accepted and went unknowing that the loud music, chaotic house, and the hired clown were all factors that could trigger his sensory overload. It was supposed to be a fun day for my son and an opportunity for him to engage with children of his own age. I was excited, in fact.

Only ten minutes had passed as we got there, and he was on the verge of a meltdown. By the fifteen-minute mark, we were back in the car, on our way home. I didn't understand it then; I thought it was just a phase in both of our lives. That day, I honestly thought, believed, and hoped that I could teach him to socialize with others amidst the loud noises and chaos that parties brought.

The following year, his cousin threw another birthday party. I asked my son if he wanted to go, and he didn't. I wanted him to go because I thought he was missing out. I'm not a monster; I am a mother who wants my son to spend quality time with his peers. So, this time, I was more cautious. I asked my sister to set up a zen den for him to escape if he felt overwhelmed.

However, I soon realized when talking to him that my son was happier at home. It was me who wanted him to go for fear of missing out. It took me a while to understand that he wasn't missing out at all because he was completely fine about it! That's when I learned that if my son is happy about something, even if it may seem different from what others consider normal or acceptable, then I should be too. It was challenging to comprehend at first. But with the love that I have for my son, I soon learned to accept what works best for him and not what I thought was best.

To give our children the best care that they deserve, understanding their condition is a prerequisite. We've heard a lot about autism, but what actually is high functioning autism?

Autism ranges from mild to severe depending on its symptoms. Before 2013, only those with severe symptoms were diagnosed with autism, but as studies progressed, autism has been classified into three levels, collectively being called Autism Spectrum Disorder (ASD). High-functioning autism is a level within this neurodevelopmental spectrum that sits on the higher end. This means that children and adults with HFA experience different symptoms than others. They can usually speak, write, and live independently, yet they have difficulties in social interaction, communication skills, and self-regulation.

Children with high functioning autism can go years without a diagnosis; however, it is common for children to be diagnosed later into elementary school. My son was not diagnosed until he was 6, although it was clear that he was neurologically different from 18 months. In general, most symptoms such as lack of social interaction and social development skills don't typically show up until they start preschool or elementary school, where they are required to interact with other children.

At the start of my parenting journey, I asked many questions: "How can I better understand my child's needs?" "How can I help them improve their social interaction?" "How can I teach them to communicate well?" are questions that occupied my mind once too, and I realized, being a mother to a HFA child requires more love, more patience, more focus, and a long thread of understanding.

As a mother of a child with high-functioning autism, I deeply understand how it is to raise them. The constant struggles -- day in, day out, the days and nights when you feel overwhelmed, stressed out, or somehow guilty for not being a better parent -- are all stages that I have gone through. It isn't easy, trying to solve one situation only to go forward to another. Yet, if there is one crucial thing that I have learned along the way, it is to treat every circumstance as a ladder. Every time I learn some-thing, I go up one step.

Seeing them suffer from anxiety is a painful view, and what hurts worse is learning that these symptoms are typical for our children with HFA. It is saddening and heartbreaking to find out that you know where it aches, but you do not exactly know how to ease their pain. It is sometimes difficult to admit to ourselves or to anyone else that we are struggling or that there are times when we want to cry with them, wishing we could do better. But let me tell you something -- *it's okay.*

It is okay to cry at times. It is alright to admit that it is difficult because it is indeed. Our children may be strug-gling in some aspects, and that is exactly why we are working harder. It is okay to pause at times and ask for help and guidance, because why should we not? We are all parents who want to understand our children better.

As parents of HFA children, we face social anxieties and difficulties every single day. We experience their unexpected meltdowns; we witness unusual behaviors, we are baffled by their inappropriate reactions, such as extreme displays of emotions or the lack of it. Or for some children, they may be acting younger than their actual age, and we call them by their name, but they are unresponsive --these are just some of the challenges that we regularly face with our children. It can be overwhelming but remember that each child within the spectrum is unique, and each child manifests a different set of symptoms. Collectively, we should practice patience and deep understanding and seek advice and study solutions from experts, parents, or teachers who are experiencing the same. You and your child are on a journey that you are taking hand in hand, and many other people are taking this path with you, including myself.

Often, our situation may seem frustrating, and most times, exhausting. But what we shouldn't forget is that they are battling with us too, along with many other HFA children, parents, grandparents, guardians, or teachers. We are all aiming to understand the uniqueness of our child with HFA.

Understanding Your High Functioning Autistic Child will answer your questions and worries about your HFA child. I know that there are days when you feel you are walking blindfolded, not knowing what to do during meltdowns, or incapable of comprehending why they are exhibiting unwanted behaviors. These moments are precisely what this book is for, to help you understand them further, nurture them better, and guide them through the best they can be, all while being the most incredible parent you can imagine. This book will outline the first steps for parents who have a newly diagnosed high functioning autistic child, providing solutions to common problems that we all share. In this book, you will find practical, hands-on strategies and tools you can use to help you and your child thrive. Moreover, it will help you understand your child's needs with a detailed approach to improve their communication and social interaction while overcoming the shared challenges for parents of HFA children.

The advice and tips compiled in this book are all things I wish I had learned early on. You will discover our children's common interests, weaknesses, and strengths that we can study further and use to their advantage. As a parent who struggled with my HFA child in the early stage of his diagnosis, I have learned that positive parenting matters to me a lot. Therefore, this book will not only be your guide to understanding your HFA child but as your companion in your journey -- *our journey* that we are taking with our children.

Being a mother to a HFA child, patience is often the biggest test, especially when you are on the brink of a breakdown. I am thankful to have overcome the trials of patience (albeit, there were times when I did lose it!), which is why I want to share the learnings I have gathered along the way. Parenting isn't easy as it is, and for my three children, parenting was more complicated than I anticipated. My eldest son is HFA, my second son has Attention-deficit/Hyperactivity Disorder (ADHD), and my youngest daughter is dyslexic. They all required more support and focus growing up, and I know how difficult it is to navigate *this* world. It can be lonesome and stressful for us parents, and often, all we need is an occasional thumbs up or a pat on the back, making us feel that we're not alone and a helping hand that will guide us along.

I created this guide to help you as you go through the similar things I did and shed light on advice I wish someone had told me before. I know and understand all the ups and downs, the uncertain days, the times when our anxieties drown us, the days when we want to cry it all out, and everything in between. Apart from parenting my three children, I have also taught in mainstream and special needs schools, where I have learned more situations than I have ever encountered with my children. This is also where I realized that our HFA children are unique in their own quirky and wonderful ways, and none of them are the same.

I have learned to love my son's autism and all the peculiarity that comes with it because, to be honest, I cannot imagine life any different now.

ILLUSTRATION

The Autism spectrum has three known levels reflecting its severity, numbering each level from 1 to 3, using one (1) as the mildest. These three levels determine the intensity of support each child needs.

The Three Levels of Autism
(from an autistic perspective)

Level 1	Level 2	Level 3
Requiring support	**Requiring substantial support**	**Requiring very substantial support**
• I need help in coursing through an environment with neuro-typicals... • People see me as annoying, because of my sudden movements and little quirks. • They say I'm weird and awkward, even though I try my best not to be. They don't see me as disabled. • I can make friends with neurotypical children, but it's often a struggle. • I can talk and communicate, but not too well. I have trouble in back-and-forth conversations. • I prefer routine over change.	• I need support in navigating through day-to-day challenges... • My behaviors are unusual, and I typically have repetitive practices. • People often easily figure out that I am disabled. • I have trouble making friends. I have a very limited social life and possess very narrow interests. • I can only speak in very simple sentences, and I have difficulties in communicating non-verbally. • I find it hard to accept change, and I get easily upset when I need to move from one activity to another.	• I need full-time support and a high level of understanding... • My behavior is greatly unusual, and I usually do repetitive practices to calm myself. • People take one look at me and know I am disabled. • Social interaction is almost non-existent for me. I can't express myself in any way, and I rarely initiate interactions. • My ability to communicate is very limited. I typically speak only when asked or when I need something. • I can't handle change and transitions. Change is a difficult and unbearable endeavor for me.

What you don't know is that...	*What you don't know is that...*	*What you don't know is that...*
• I have difficulties in interacting socially with peers. • I can mask my own symptoms, but not always. And it's a constant struggle. • Reaching other people's standards is exhausting, so please understand as much as you can.	• I may not be as responsive and attentive as others, but I understand what you say about me. • Those unusual behaviors and repetitive practices help me feel comfortable, safe, and less anxious. • Stress is a constant concern and I need support to cope with it.	• You may call me, and I wouldn't answer, but that doesn't mean I couldn't hear and understand you. • Those unusual behaviors and repetitive practices help me feel comfortable, safe, and less anxious. • Communication is a near-impossible endeavor and I need a great deal of support.
• I need support, not hate.	• I need support, not hate.	• I need support, not hate.

These symptoms and levels are not definite. A number of factors like the environment, the people they interact with, stress, and the type and level of support they experience can seriously influence their capability to function and live well.

1

YOU ARE NOT ALONE!

Over the years, I have cried with mothers, comforted relatives, and empathized with grandparents who, like me, are guardians of children with HFA. It took me years to overcome the daily struggles. I didn't just wake up one day and realize I finally had it all figured out. I did not skip all the hurdles and sleepless nights wondering what went wrong. What I did was wake up every morning looking for answers to new situations and continuously trying to learn new things that I was not yet aware of. I went through it step by step, taking each day at a time.

A friend of mine from a support group I attended once cried because her son would not let her hug him. It was painful to hear, not only for the thought of not having the child you had wished for but for feeling guilty somehow and thinking that whatever we do, we can never be enough for them. There are times that we blame ourselves as their parents. We feel like something could have been done for them earlier, and the blaming gets worse when we start putting it on someone else. First of all, it is unhealthy to blame yourself. Second, you shouldn't blame your partner or relatives either. So, please, do not blame anyone.

Grieving is a normal phase everybody goes through when they first learn about their child's condition. Everybody grieves, and it is natural and essential. It indicates that we care more than we realize. Many parents feel guilty during these times, but we should always keep in mind that it is not wrong to ask for help and seek the therapy we need.

What does the grieving process mean, anyway? For us, grieving is not saying that our child is not normal. Grieving does not mean we perceive our child as "less than" the others. Grieving most definitely does not mean we love them less. This phase we go through only means that we acknowledge that the journey we had hoped to walk with our child will look different now. Every corner, every avenue, every hallway of it, is going to be different.

Many people will frown upon the grieving process because they do not understand what we are going through. All the birthdays that we planned, holidays, school gatherings, education, and even family bondings will be different. Everything that we had envisioned before they were born is now just a figment of our past thoughts. Many parents feel discouraged upon hearing the word "autism" the first time their child is diagnosed. You must know, grieving is ok and, more importantly, nothing to be ashamed of.

It's not your fault

The first stage of grief is guilt. Whenever we receive unprecedented news, we try to process things first and then blame ourselves afterward. So when we first learn that our child has HFA, we often look back into the past to find something we may have done wrong. We think back to our pregnancy, what we did wrong during each trimester, or we believe that perhaps this is some punishment of some sort. But none of this is true. Having a child on the spectrum doesn't point back to something we did or did not do in the past. In order to go past this, you have to believe first that *it is not your fault*.

Recreating dreams

Before I conceived my son, I had an array of hopes

and dreams for him, and my family being very sporty; we had always imagined our children being part of team sports. It is normal for us parents to have their whole lives figured out even before they are born. We envision ourselves walking with them by the park, watching them ride bikes and play kites, and nurturing them into better individuals than ourselves. Yet, once we learn about their condition, a vast majority of those plans seem to shatter. Do not punish yourself for feeling this way. Your family will face a whole new world with new and exciting possibilities that may seem different at first, but you will soon embrace the new. There will be times where you will be uncertain, nervous, and over-whelmed, although if you remain in a stage of blaming yourself or your partner, you will not be able to move forward into creating a new world for your loved ones. With the tools outlined in this book, you will learn how to adapt to the changes ahead.

Once you accept that your parenting journey looks different, you can begin to relish in the new world you will create. We re-evaluate our plans for them, and we recreate the dreams we once had. For instance, you always hoped that your child would be a social butterfly, but now that you know they are on the spectrum, you realize that being overtly social will be a struggle and a hindrance for them. Like my son's cousin's birthday story, you have to evaluate what is best for your child as a parent. They may not grow to be overly social, but instead, they may grow to be a wizard in chess. It is natural to have high dreams for our children. Who doesn't? We want them to grow up even better than us. There is no reason for this not to be the case. Irrespective of the challenges you will face, if you care for them and nurture them well, there is every possibility they can attain better than what you initially hoped for.

It's okay to ask for help

It is normal to go through all the stages of grief, which is why there is a chapter dedicated to this particular element of parenting. However, as parents, we have to move forward, and we have to get up each day and learn how to help our children thrive. We have to make them feel that they are not alone because we are not as well. When I finally accepted my son's diagnosis, I read, researched, and studied how I could help as a mother. My children are in their late teens now, which requires a very different understanding to when they were in elementary school! So, I am still learning. As I have said countless times, none of our HFA children are the same. And I did not go through this journey figuring things out alone. I sought help from books, experts, and therapies.

Therapists are a huge resource for you and your child. Oftentimes, we will feel overwhelmed by the issues we have on our plate, as navigating *this* new world can be challenging. Seeking therapy is a resource all parents are entitled to. Experiencing bursts of disproportionate rage, resentment, and an overwhelming feeling you cannot go on can lead to you becoming socially distanced from your loved ones, which is why, if you feel like this, you should speak to a professional.

Sometimes, we are afraid to show weakness or ashamed to let others know that we cannot manage. Most people fear therapy because they are embarrassed to acknowledge they need them, except having the ability to express yourself freely without judgment will benefit you and your child extensively.

If you acknowledge you need therapy, you'll learn more about yourself. Therapy can unlock understanding, alter perspective and rekindle gratitude. The ability to discuss your pains and struggles in a safe environment can provide the support required to persevere with more success. A significant benefit of pursuing professional help is the direction it can provide, which, more often than not, can be lost at times. An hour a week away from your family may be the answer to alleviate your stressors; as you are constantly worrying about theirs, some alone time to concentrate on yourself is critical for your well-being. Engaging with therapy can help you improve on all parts of your life, including your relationships with your partner, which can put a strain on intimate relationships, especially when you are both struggling with raising your HFA child. Therapies can alleviate guilt or resentment that may be lingering, but most importantly, they can make you discover what is holding you back from taking action to create change.

Meet new friends on the same journey

Another essential factor that can positively impact your parenting is joining support groups for parents of HFA children. In the first few weeks or months after your child's diagnosis, you might feel alone and isolated because you do not know any other parents in the same position as you. Once you explore the support groups available, you'll realize there are a lot of parents struggling like you, and you will be amazed to see how many there are. Especially now in the digital age, it's pretty easy to connect with other people, far or near. Join support groups online and in real life to meet other parents on the same journey as you. There, you will find parents who will be supportive of your growth as a neophyte in *this* world, and you will come across the most up-to-date information coming from firsthand experiences of real-life HFA parents.

Aside from the new data and knowledge you will encounter along the way, bonding with like-minded parents will be fun! You will have a listening ear to express your difficulties without the fear of being judged. Better yet, you will have someone to talk to about your child's little quirks and all the things they do that most parents may see as awkward, but for us parents with little ones on the spectrum, they just get it.

While collecting all the information you can in seeking answers, not all will be effective for your child. Nevertheless, do not be discouraged. As the parent of your child, you are the one who knows your child best, which means you are the only person who has the power to filter what can help your child and what cannot. Some HFA children can be extremely sensitive to emotions, while others can be clueless about expressing themselves. As their parent, you are often the translator, interpreter, and moderator because you spend the most time with them and understand them more than anyone. For this reason, don't believe everything you read, and be selective of what information you embrace and what you think is relevant for your child. You may receive tips from other parents in support groups, but not all that works for their children will work for yours. You will learn new strategies from experts, but by the end of the day, you will have to undergo experiments and tests on your own to see if the newly acquired knowledge works for your child. The point is, you have to trust your gut, always, because of all people, you know your child the most.

Redefine what is "normal"

One of the most common errors for parents of children with any form of autism is to compare your child to neurotypical children. It is hard to get out of this phase because not everyone understands how it affects our children and also us parents. To start your journey into becoming a positive parent, you must first redefine "normal." What does normal mean for us parents with a HFA child?

Redefining normal starts with your perspective - - *your mindset.* Navigating life as a HFA child in a neuro-typical world is undoubtedly challenging, but as long as we see them as a child no less than others, a son or a daughter who only needs more care and support, they can live their lives no more different than their peers.

They hear and understand us, so in whatever you do, you should treat them and make them feel that they belong. Never talk about your child like they are not in the room because they can hear and understand you. The same goes for comparing them with children, which other parents and children will inevitably do. If there is anyone who will compare them to others, it should not be you. Do not let anyone underestimate or under-support your child. As parents, we must be their first line of defense when they are put in unpleasant situations. This is not being overprotective either; it is called caring for and supporting your child.

Patience is a virtue, but understanding with empathy is a skill. They may have difficulties completing tasks that are too simple for their age, but instead of pressuring them and getting disappointed, we need to encourage and accompany them all the way. Understand, because this condition is not something that "they will just grow out of." Do not use HFA as an excuse for their bad behavior either. Remember that we are looking for lessons to help our children cope with everyday life, including teaching them how to behave appropriately. Always keep in mind that you *can* manage. It may be difficult at times, overwhelming even. But you have the skills, the patience, and determination, to get through this in one piece.

Lastly, do not be phased when people judge you nor care about your child appearing normal. These are the things that can be part of our battle, but we do not have to listen. In fact, we should not listen at all. In his first week of school, I once taught a young boy in Grade 1 who refused to leave his cave (safe space at home). He found true comfort in Spiderman. So, his dad dressed up as Spiderman every day for a week to take his child to school. It was the confidence boost that the child needed to leave the house and go to school. However, it was an absolute nightmare for his dad, as he had to go home using public transport by himself, which gave him a lot of unwanted attention! The bottom line is we should be the first soldiers for our children, even if it means going beyond the line and exerting extra effort for them to grow. HFA children will get unwanted attention, but that should not be a reason for us to be discouraged. Never forget that our children are gifts to cherish, albeit weird and wonderful!

Certainly, it will be overwhelming and sometimes frustrating, but there will be a lot of help along the way. I think the best advice that really stuck with me is "Be patient with your child and with yourself. Live one day at a time," and I guess it can never be more accurate. Our life is like a book. If we skip through to the end to see the answer to our questions, we would have skipped the learning in between. Do not try to fix all things at once. It is a life-long journey, and progress will take time.

Along the way, we will find answers, and we will watch how they progress, one step at a time.

It is easy to say, "This is so hard!" in the beginning because it is indeed a struggle. You are on a journey with different challenges and a different kind of joy from what you are used to, but as your child grows, you will too. You will learn to see the quirky, warming, and definitely funny side of things on this journey very quickly.

2

THE FIRST 5 STEPS AFTER THE DIAGNOSIS

Receiving the diagnosis can be a daunting and overwhelming experience. The future may seem blurry; however, you have to overcome the uncertainties to guide your child along the right path. As a parent, you have to be strong to attend to your child's needs properly. After the grieving process, you must now redirect your focus and start to actually learn, seek answers, and help your child settle into their new normal.

Step 1 - Assemble the right team

Despite the ongoing advancements in medicine, for decades, there is still no universally accepted cure for

HFA. We must rely on decreasing stressors to make our children comfortable and support them to help improve the skills they are having difficulties with. As parents, we must endeavor to conduct our own research, talk to experts, and try therapies, all with similar goals in mind - - to alleviate our children's concerns in order to help them thrive and succeed.

After receiving the HFA diagnosis and going through the initial grieving process, you should then move on and start planning how to help your child navigate the world. To do that, you must first recognize that all HFA children have varying needs, and you will learn that throughout the pages of this book. We have to develop a unique program that is specifically designed for our children. In short, we have to assemble a team of professionals and experts to give the best to our children. I will not give you a list of my son's therapies because what worked for my child may not work for yours. Instead, you should pick out the traits you see in your child with what you read throughout this chapter to create a set of treatments and approaches that would give the best result for your HFA child. Most importantly, remember that despite their differences, our children have something in common -- they all need extra love and support, where we, parents, are required most.

. . .

Speech Therapy

If your child demonstrates speech and language difficulties such as: having a hard time expressing their emotions, difficulty understanding facial expressions and other's tone of voice, trouble comprehending metaphors and sarcasm, or problems with starting or ending conversations -- then Speech and Language Therapy (SLT) can help your child.

Speech and language, delays, and communication difficulties can hinder our children from participating and appreciating social events or gatherings in their lives. For instance, they may make a teacher or a friend upset but not realize it because facial expression or tone of voice did not give them any helpful cue. This can hamper their chances of making friends because it can often create barriers when new relationships are forming. This is especially true of our children that are literal thinkers; comprehending jokes is often non-existent.

Seek speech therapies that undergo assessments in a variety of settings, both formally and informally. At home and in school are good places to start for the therapist to gather sufficient information on your child's skills or difficulties they are experiencing. Once initial assessments are complete, therapy can commence.

Attention and listening therapy is a common type

that aims to increase attention, concentration, and ability to follow instructions. If your child struggles to attend to one activity or sit for long periods of time and struggles with direction, this particular avenue of SLT could be an option for your child. The therapy should be one-to-one and bespoke to your child's needs. Attention and listening therapy can provide your child with the critical skills for social interaction, play, and language skills.

Receptive language therapy is particularly pertinent for HFA children as it targets their misunderstanding of vocabulary and sentence complexity, facilitating their academic learning. Many HFA children have a literal understanding paired with a difficulty inferring information, so the speech and language therapist may use comics, pictures, books, and video clips to ascertain a more focused approach for each child.

Overall, speech and language therapy aims to increase your child's skill base to reduce their frustrations. If seeking SLT ensure the therapy is tailored to your child's needs, and do not be afraid to ask the therapist what you can do at home to replicate therapy to better their skills. Only this way can therapy truly result in increased independence and improved confidence.

Cognitive Behavioral Therapy

One of the most common approaches for children with HFA is Cognitive behavior therapy (CBT). It addresses the secondary issues related to autism, such as bullying, stress, anger, emotional regulation, and anxiety among HFA children. It is a psychotherapeutic treatment that helps children identify disturbing thought patterns that can negatively affect their behavior. Through CBT, HFA children can turn these patterns into positive thoughts, equipping them for social interactions.

CBT works by targeting the factors that give your child anxiety. It addresses negative thoughts that can cause additional stress for your child and then transforms or replaces them with better ones. This process changes how they perceive the things around them.

This brings us to the question, how would we know if our child needs CBT?

CBT would benefit HFA children who suffer from depression and anxiety, two conditions that commonly co-exist with HFA. Depression and anxiety may seem like big calls for a child under 10, but it is not uncommon. If you are unsure, there are common signs of anxiety and depression to look out for. Suppose your child begins to consistently avoid situations due to social pressure, or they exert a specific phobia or irrational fear that poses little or no actual danger, such as alarms at school or being scared of the dark. Another sign to look out for is separation anxiety. If your child separates from attachment figures (such as you) and evokes extreme avoidance behaviors or they are having regular emotional outbursts, this could be managed with CBT. Similarly, another common sign/symptom to watch out for would be if your child displays intense levels of distress when their environment or routine changes. If your child happens to experience these, then you would find CBT extremely helpful.

CBT can develop our children's coping mechanisms and manage their reactions to different situations with its short-term and problem-focused approach. CBT comprises behavioral strategies such as social skills training, role play, relaxation, and conflict resolution, which has an overall aim to alleviate the burden of anxiety and depression to our children. To us parents, it can give us a better understanding of our children's experiences and fears.

Social Integration Therapy

HFA is generally characterized by deficits in communication skills and social interaction. These two are hallmarks of HFA, and most of our children share these difficulties. People in the medical field call this "social blindness," which indicates their inability to see and understand social cues that, as parents we know intuitively, like indications of ownership on things, jokes, sarcasm, the meaning behind people's specific tone of voice, and such. Sadly, HFA children are more likely to experience social blindness.

The good news is they can work it out! Therapists, physicians, and other field experts have a multitude of ways to help our children overcome these challenges, and they call it social integration skills training.

Social integration therapies are composed of activities that will help your child understand how social interaction with others works. This approach aims to break down and analyze social skills and teach them step by step in their most basic form. Most of our HFA children perceive literal meanings behind nonliteral language, such as figures of speech, so these therapies are usually done gradually, depending on one's age. For instance, a five-year-old HFA can be taught how to share toys with their playmates. Then, as the child grows older, the basic skills will branch out into more complex social skills, such as interacting within school scenarios or initiating conversations in group settings.

· · ·

Social integration therapy techniques

- One of the techniques involved in the training is providing them with personally made **comic strips** to help them understand different social situations. These are typically situational stories showing the positive social responses a child can take in any given situation. A child with HFA in the story will display the reactions a HFA child would typically do while presenting what the other characters in the story are thinking about. This will illuminate how other people perceive their reactions and how they can alter their negative responses. Then, the therapist or physician can teach them the more appropriate reactions when such situations arise in their actual day-to-day life.

- Social integration therapy also employs the "**hidden curriculum**," an approach that aims to teach our HFA children the "unspoken" rules of social interaction. These include the unwritten guidelines or customs in the social sphere that we know by instinct. For example, when a certain seat in

the classroom has already been occupied
and there are belongings on top of the desk,
we quickly recognize that the seat is taken
even if the person is not around. A HFA
child often misses out on these apparent
indications. Often, they would think that
the seat is available, so they would sit on it,
causing conflicts with other children
without them knowing or even
understanding what they did wrong. We
don't want our children to be labeled 'rude'
or considered to have bad behavior.

This is where the hidden curriculum benefits our children. This strategy teaches them social cues, breaking them down into simple components that our HFA children can easily understand. Some of the most fundamental areas of the hidden curriculum include the proper and polite ways to talk in class, how to dress appropriately depending on a situation, interrupting people, or the right time to discuss their opinions and say what they think...which is often a challenge when most HFA children have no filter!

- Another technique used in this therapy is called **social scripts**, which shouldn't be mistaken with the aforementioned social stories. In this technique, HFA children are taught scripted phrases they can use in real-life conversations with peers. Lines such as "Do you like playing with toy cars?" are given to them to help them initiate conversations. HFA children are often offered reminder cards for their scripts which are removed once they learn to compose questions and phrases on their own.

- **Technological interventions** such as showing videos or the use of virtual-reality programs can help HFA children build a better understanding of complex social cues. This approach aims to guide them to analyze their actions in various ways, such as watching themselves interact socially through a simulated computer program. Then, using vivid explanations, therapists will break down a child's actions and give them ideas to improve their skills further.

Occupational Therapy

Another therapy that you can look into is occupational therapy (OT). OT practitioners are often assigned in places such as child centers, daycares, or schools. Through activity participation, occupational therapists develop our children's ability to live independently by studying their development and interaction.

There are many reasons why our HFA children may not want to participate in social activities. They may feel like they don't belong or fear that they may fail to communicate. The primary purpose of OT is to modify these barriers and improve their physical, social, and cognitive disabilities.

So how does it work?

First, an occupational therapist will assess your child's abilities, including dressing and personal care tasks, motor skills, and interactions, and will most likely discuss the strengths and weaknesses you feel your child needs to work on with you as a parent. OT's can also help to develop bedtime routines which is a common struggle for any parent. My son had a particular bedtime routine that required many sessions with an OT to help eradicate unwanted behaviors. In Occupational Therapy, play-based therapy is often utilized to engage children and provide practical techniques and solutions.

Ensure to have a specifically tailored program if you pursue a treatment program with an OT.

Applied Behavior Therapy

Have you ever heard of Applied Behavior Therapy (ABA)? As a child's parent on the spectrum, I believe many of you know or are at least familiar with it. Many experts consider ABA as the gold standard in improving an autistic child's skills. It has records of a high success rate and is regarded as the most tested and well-researched method by far. This therapy aims to progress one's skills through "positive reinforcement," where good behavior is rewarded, thus encouraging HFA children to repeat those actions.

ABA is composed of several stages that are all tailored to your child's specific needs. Like in OT, the therapist will observe your child and develop a program that is aligned with your child's distinctive needs. The therapist can employ these strategies at home under your supervision, making it easier for your child to master life skills.

ABA can be implemented for 40 hours a week, which may seem excessive, although it can also be applied part-time. However, you should note that ABA is not for everyone. As ironic as it may sound, some children respond negatively to positive reinforcement. You may hear it as a frequent subject of debates and controversies because of its similarity with Pavlov's dog experiment for the reward system.

Nonetheless, ABA has a high success rate which cannot be ignored. It takes a comprehensive approach with different intricate pieces of training for varying needs. Commonly ABA is known for its use of drills, which are intense one-to-one learning of specific behaviors that are repeated to help strengthen long-term memory. If your child needs help with responsiveness to cues, motivation, and building initiative, ABA can be tightly or loosely structured to fit your child's needs. ABA aims to teach skills to replace problem behaviors and above all, maintain their behaviors by changing their responses and improving cognitive skills.

Floortime

A relatively new therapy is Floortime. As the name implies, it is an approach where a parent sits down on the floor with their HFA child to play and interact with them at their level. This aims to widen the child's "circle of communication" by increasing the number of individuals they interact with. Even though it may look simple, floortime helps develop skills and build the strengths of HFA children.

Floortime works by incorporating the intervention into playtime. For instance, parents can imitate how their children play with a doll, thus playing at the same level as their HFA children. The parent will dress up dolls too, but after a while, the parent will add complexity to the game by adding conversations that will reflect on areas of communication the child may struggle with. For example, the parent will use a doll as a character who initiates a conversation with their child's doll. This will then stimulate a response from the child, making them more perceptive of real life, habitual interactions, which in turn should promote engagement, communication, and thinking.

Respite Care for Parents

Not all therapies are intended for your child. Our children's high-functioning autism leaves us equally stressed out, drained, or overwhelmed by the challenges they face. Respite care is a service that provides you with a much-needed break from your responsibilities. This is a short-term service given to carers and parents of children, which can last for hours, days, and possibly weeks. Respite care can be costly if you are not entitled to it through the state. However, parenting a child on the spectrum can be challenging and overwhelming. You should not be ashamed to take a well-deserved break.

All the above therapies are based on your child's specific needs. Reading through the symptoms and solutions from the different types of therapy, you may have an idea by now which therapies suit your child best. If you are confused, do not feel bad either. You can always ask therapists and experts which approach is best for your child and also take into account most therapies work on a multidisciplinary approach, which simply means they work with other therapists to elicit the best results for each child. They are experts in the field who have encountered countless HFA children like our own, so all we have to do is trust and ask them.

Communicate with professionals to further your understanding. Yet, also be assertive when selecting the practitioners when assembling your team. If you are unsure about any practitioner, do not be afraid to ask them about their experience with children on the spectrum; likewise, you should not hesitate to ask for references.

Note that therapies' rates vary depending on your U.S. state or country. Private facilities and public assistance also differ considerably in rates. If possible, you can start contacting insurance companies, or if you have insurance to claim through work, you should speak to your HR department.

Step 2: Gain firsthand knowledge

To fully understand our HFA children, we should interact and seek answers not only from the experts but from HFA adults themselves. "The field beats the books," as the saying goes. HFA adults have firsthand experience on how complex our children's situations are, and having gone through the same phase, and they will be able to offer suggestions and input on how to give our HFA children a better life experience.

Utilizing HFA adults can shed light on the types of therapies that worked best for them with honest positives and negatives alongside accommodations for specific stressors you may not have thought of. Speaking with HFA adults can explain how each intervention works when applied in real life. You can think of this approach as gathering honest reviews from people from the same point of view as your child.

Step 3: Embrace the 'atypical'

There is always this constant urge at the back of our

minds telling us to encourage our HFA children to play with others, interact and make friends, or go out and spend time with their peers. That is what we did as children, and that is what the norm tells us to expect. Urging them to "fit in" and ignoring their preferences can overwhelm and pressure them. For this reason, the best thing to do as parents is to accept what makes them happy.

In the introduction, I shared a personal story about how I feared my son was missing out, so I drove him to a loud party to socialize. What I didn't know back then was he was happier being at home. Our home was his comfort zone, so who am I to ignore that? The lesson from my story is that we should remember that their happiness is always more important than our expectations as parents. It is normal to plan things out for our children, but if we limit our perception of them within our expectations, they will never supersede them. Worse, it could affect their self-esteem. Support them on their own definition of happiness, embrace them for who they are, and do not pressure them to "fit in."

Step 4: Be honest about their condition

Many parents are afraid to label their children with HFA because they may use this as an excuse not to work hard and to give up easily on challenges they may face in life. However, telling your child they are on the spectrum of autism is essential. I still dread the day that my child will say, "I can't do it, I have autism," or "Isn't that too hard for a HFA child like me?" But as much as we worry about these things, we also want them to be knowledgeable of their condition and understand that they are special early on.

Another concern amongst us parents is the fear that knowing their condition could make our children feel different or broken. To be honest, this was one of my greatest fears. Ironically, I learned from HFA adults that knowing their condition early on drove them toward their goals. None of us know how it may turn out for our children, but with our support and guidance, they can reach their highest potential.

You may be asking now, "When is the right time to tell them?" This is entirely up to you as their parent, although on average, children are not diagnosed until they are 6 or 7, which means they probably already know they are slightly different. Having a conversation about the umbrella term 'spectrum' will help them understand the world better, cope with their diagnosis, and even drive them to become the best version of themself. By concealing this crucial information, we prevent them from understanding, accepting, and appreciating their uniqueness. Imagine raising your child without them knowing why they cannot interact as smoothly as others or why they cannot comprehend ideas as quickly as their peers. More likely, this would lead to feelings of indifference, and they will grow to isolate themselves, damaging their self-esteem, which could lead to them feeling like they are a failure.

Sit them down and discuss what it means to be a high-functioning autistic child. Watch videos, read blogs, articles and take your child to group autism sessions for them to be able to relate and recognize they are not alone. Ensure this conversation is had at the right time, with plenty of opportunities for questions and queries to be answered in a calm environment. Above all, this conversation must be between you and your child with no other siblings in the room, and most certainly, do not tell siblings before you have told your HFA child. Be understanding that your child may be a little confused or disheartened with the diagnosis, although partnered with guidance and loving support, your child will come to accept their newfound identity and thrive.

Step 5: Tell professionals

Meeting a pediatrician or a dentist for the first time

can be upsetting or scary, and our HFA children may freak out unexpectedly. We wouldn't want to handle a meltdown in those settings because aside from causing inconveniences to both parties, it may also harm our children or the healthcare provider. To avoid this problem, be sure to inform professionals about your child's condition ahead of time. This is especially important if your child needs to interact with the person directly. Doing so can help them manage their expectations and carry out advance preparation to accommodate our children more delicately if need be.

For example, if we tell our children's dentist about their condition, the dentist will make adjustments and additional measures to make our child comfortable. They may explain what is going to happen in explicit detail or if the process will cause discomfort. Phrases like, "I'm going to turn on the drill now" or "I'm going to spray this water inside your mouth, tell me if you want me to stop" will surely help your child trust the professional and make them feel comfortable.

————

The support we provide at the beginning of their journey is the most important, as early intervention can decrease unwanted behaviors and, in some cases, revert them completely. It will seem overwhelming at first, but there will always be people that will help us out. Professionals, experts, therapists, teachers, books, and even HFA adults themselves, are everywhere. So it is important to follow these steps to give your child the best available. In the end, the most important thing is that you are present as a parent, and you seek the best possible intervention with a goal to improve your child's skills and wellbeing.

3

THREE STRATEGIES TO UNDERSTAND YOUR CHILD BETTER

W hen my son was first diagnosed, I can say that the most challenging part was understanding his needs. I had trouble understanding his mannerisms, behaviors, and expressions. There were times when he would be extremely sensitive, and I had no idea how to deal with it. I was clueless about how I could accommodate his needs at home. I realized back then that the most significant barrier between my child and me was communication. So, I tried to adjust and look outside the box for tips and advice on how I could comprehend his nonverbal cues, and it surprised me to discover a long list of things we can do now to understand our children better.

. . .

1. Understanding expression of emotion

We parents need to put in extra time and effort when it comes to understanding our HFA children. Showing their feelings is not always easy for them, especially when they are expressing themselves nonverbally. Their nonverbal cues, such as crying, can be almost impossible to analyze when trying to determine their triggers. A good place to start is to allow your child extra processing time when given instructions or when expecting a response.

This extra time alleviates pressure put on your child to process things quicker than they are capable. Perhaps it will be a couple of minutes, or maybe only 30 seconds extra is needed for your child to keep up with any given situation. Allowing this time will also decrease stress or anxiety for you. As a result of getting a little space and some extra time to process their thoughts, there is a smaller likelihood of you losing your patience because they were taking too long!

To further understand your child, you must participate in harnessing their skills. Aside from the therapies mentioned above involving us (like floortime), teaching them by ourselves about problem-solving skills can help our children understand social norms and at the same time make them trust us as their mentor and companion. Training them with problem-solving skills not only teaches our HFA children how to react to different situations but also to sharpen their social understanding and cognition as well.

Developing "Theory of Mind"

Children usually develop what they call a "theory of mind" growing up, which refers to a child's ability to understand and acknowledge that not everyone shares the same thoughts and feelings as them. For our HFA child, this ability, along with problem-solving skills, is often learned at a later age. However, there are a few strategies that you can use to aid your child in developing theory of mind sooner.

First, you must explain to your child what different facial expressions look like and what they often mean. This way, your child can have an idea of what expressions to expect and what not to. Talking aloud about your thoughts and feelings will also help them recognize what each feeling stands for and what causes they are associated with. For instance, you can tell your child that you are hungry because you have not eaten anything yet. The feeling of hunger will be associated with not eating, which they should understand and remember. Being vocal and clearly linking your vocabulary to your emotions will teach your child how to do the same.

We can engage them in the conversation by asking them questions that will test their newly acquired knowledge, like asking them, "How about you, are you hungry?" This will raise a question to them where they will try to seek an answer. Another effective technique you can use is using "cognitive verbs" frequently while speaking or doing daily activities with your child. Cognitive verbs such as "think, feel, wonder, or imagine" can trigger your child's responses and expose them to thoughts and ideas. "I wonder how tall that tree is?" "I imagine there is life on other planets" Use your words as much as possible to illustrate to your child that making conversation is easy and a good thing!

Consistently talking about other people's feelings can also help them develop theory of mind. You can tell your child about the things that they like, and others do not. For instance, you can talk about how your child loves mascots whilst their friend doesn't. Tell them why and how their reactions are different when they see one. This will help your child understand that as people we all feel differently towards things -- and that is ok.

· · ·

Speech Bubbles

Another resource to help with the expression of emotion is speech bubbles. A method for filtering 'what to think' and 'what to say' out loud can be illustrated through drawing bubbles. You can draw two figures, your child and a peer or someone they know, having a conversation. Using speech bubbles will help emphasize the difference between what one is thinking and what one actually says. An example would be drawings of your child talking to a classmate, saying, "Your shoes look good on you," instead of "I don't like your shoes." Explain to them that there is a fine line between complete honesty and being socially polite. This will be confusing for them initially, so you have to be patient, draw as many situations as you can think of, and most importantly, do this consistently to monitor improvement. Make this a habit or a type of play with your child and dedicate extra time to this activity.

Problem-solving skills

Children with HFA usually have difficulties solving problems that are new or have never encountered before. Problem-solving skills include knowing what will happen next, stating opinions and conclusions on their own, sequencing events that took place, and more.

To help them develop these skills, we must work through the problems with them and use questions like "What happened to the melted ice?" and "Why did it happen?" I mirrored this framework from therapy at home as it focused on helping him structure his thinking in order to answer the step-by-step questions involved in problem-solving.

First, define the problem. Ask your child to explain what happened and how the affected person (or the child themself) feels. Next, analyze it. Give your child questions like "Which happened first and last?" or "Why do you think that happened?" Once they figure out and analyze the problem, you will then proceed to generate solutions. Ask your child what they think is best to resolve what happened; you may need to guide the thought process a little to offer meaningful solutions. Then, after laying out possible solutions, you may ask them to analyze each one and choose the one that would work best, based on their analysis. It may be something as simple as a glass of water dropping and spilling on the floor, and your child is deliberating on what to do. You may need to steer their thoughts to grabbing paper towels to clean it up, but providing that vocal support will reinforce the correct behaviors for the future.

. . .

Echolalia

Your child keeps repeating what you say; whether it be words, phrases, questions, or instructions, they imitate what they hear. This is called echolalia. Children with echolalia repeat phrases that they hear, which may hinder how they communicate with others because they are not able to express their own thoughts fully. For instance, when someone asks them a question, they will repeat the question instead of answering it. Echolalia can be immediate, repeating the recently heard sounds or phrases right away, or delayed, when a child repeats what they heard hours or days after hearing it. This is common for children who are just learning to speak and communicate.

There are different reasons why a HFA child experiences echolalia even at a later age. One of which is because they learn language differently. Typically, children learn to speak words by understanding single words first, like the meaning of eat, sleep, play, write, and so on. Upon learning what each word means, they will tie them all together to create a sentence. For instance, they learned the words "I," "want," and "eat" at separate points in time. Later on, they will learn to string these words together and say, "I want to eat."

. . .

What Do Repetitive Phrases Indicate?

Our children with HFA do not usually learn the same way; instead, they try to speak in larger groups of words or phrases which they cannot break down into smaller fragments. They find it hard to put these small parts all together or even jumble them, so they only associate every sentence with how they understand a single word. For example, instead of saying the example above, they will say, "I eat." Based on their past experiences, they have already learned that the word "eat" has something to do with the act of eating. However, they fail at recognizing words such as "I" or "want" and cannot use these words individually in other sentences. We can help our HFA children overcome this by breaking each sentence up and teaching them the meaning of words one by one.

Another possible reason behind echolalia is anxiety. Most HFA children use repetitive phrases to feel more comfortable and to soothe themselves from upsetting events. However, some children repeat words to send a message as well. Frequently, HFA children may repeat the question we asked them rather than answering "yes." For instance, instead of saying "yes" to our question, "Do you want some ice cream?" they will just repeat the word "ice cream" as that is the only association they gained from your question.

Echolalia can also be a good start for your child's progress. Researchers noticed that repetition soon progresses in children with HFA, and it more often serves as a stepping stone to fluent speaking and listening. As time progresses, your HFA child will understand each fragment of phrases they would usually blankly echo and will soon learn how to combine these words to create more concrete sentences that may be jumbled at first. Gradually, phrases will be used appropriately as their understanding increases, and language will be more coherent and understandable.

Most HFA children grow out of it. However, it can lead to scripting, whereby you and your child will enter into the same dialogue in specific scenarios. It is a form of echolalia, as it is a repetitive response and a type of sensory behavior, which gives them internal satisfaction. Scripting conversations is not dangerous, or self-injurious for children, however it can limit further opportunities for skills development and independence in the long run.

We all engage in repetitive behaviors, such as cracking our knuckles when nervous orbiting our fingernails. However, we also know when the right time is to engage in those repetitive behaviors. Teaching your child when to engage in their scripting will happen if you embed communication opportunities into your daily routine; model the correct behaviors and lots of positive reinforcement as much as possible.

As for my son, he used to say the exact same thing before going to bed when he was four. I would have to respond with the same exact response every night; otherwise, he wouldn't be able to sleep. The routine was regimented. I played the same playlist of 5 songs, tucked him into bed from left to right, and said, "Goodnight sweetie, sweet dreams" (In that precise order). We didn't try to change his scripting as he grew out of it after some time.

HFA, OCD, and PANS

At first glance, high-functioning autism and **Obsessive-Compulsive Disorder (OCD)** are diagnoses that are not similar to each other. Yet, based on most symptoms manifested within each, the two are often entangled or misdiagnosed. Researchers have long found an overlap between the two, such as symptoms like repetitive behaviors. However, it is also a possibility to be diagnosed with both autism and OCD.

On the other hand, **pediatric acute-onset neuropsychiatric syndrome (PANS)** is a diagnostic category that characterizes sudden drastic changes in behavior due to an inflamed part of the brain. This condition can include symptoms like screaming, crying for hours, furiously asking for help without stating what is wrong, rejection of their favorite food and wetting the bed. Sometimes, we may relate our HFA child's behavior to the symptoms of PANS. However, it is crucial to understand that HFA symptoms are likely to appear in other conditions too. In HFA, it is normal to have nervous tics due to anxiety. Sometimes, they will wet their bed, pick their skin, or grind their teeth, but that doesn't necessarily mean our children have PANS. This may indicate another common symptom in HFA - being highly sensitive to one's environment.

CBD gummies

Aside from the natural ways of calming our HFA child, there are also products that we can use to help our child overcome overactive, anxious, or unwanted behaviors. There are products called CBD gummies and oil. These are medications that are natural remedies that can alleviate our child's symptoms. It can help them lessen anxiety, depression, and some parents say their children are calmer and more stable. It is a holistic approach that some parents may be frightened of due to its drug interactions, although there is a growing body of research to support CBD for children with ASD.

If you are considering CBD, then ensure you start with a low dosage a couple of times a day and wait at least seven days before you up the dose. If your child's symptoms and behavior heightens and becomes excessive or unmanageable for your family, a possible resolution could be to use CBD oil or gummies.

A friend in a support group tried the gummies for their 9-year-old son, which had no effect at all. However insignificant that anecdote may sound, as parents, they tried something new in an attempt to improve their child's quality of life; despite it not working, it shows positive parenting. It may or may not be something you had previously considered, although I would recommend having CBD as a viable option.

2. Sensory Sensitivity

Sometimes, our HFA child will be overly sensitive to noise or uncertain environments. This is because children with HFA usually have delicate sensory systems, making their senses easy to be overwhelmed. For instance, while it is easy for us to ignore the noisy drilling outside a classroom, the vast majority of HFA children often have difficulty shutting this sensory information down. We need to observe our children and be cautious of their environment continuously.

I remember one incident in a restaurant with my son. My family often struggled with eating inside restaurants, frequently resulting in us paying the bill early. Yet, on one particular occasion, we chose a quiet place and sat down without a hitch. Everything was going great until his meal arrived, which was fish fingers and chips -- his favorite! However, when he saw the plate of food, he instantly shut down, putting his hood over his head, and slid under the table. I did not understand it then, I thought fish fingers were his favorite. It wasn't until months later when we realized that the chips were crinkle cut instead of straight, which he was not used to and thus, couldn't handle.

Hyper- and Hypo Sensitive

Not all HFA children are highly sensitive to sensory input. Some can be hypo sensitive, which means they have low responses to these sensations and therefore crave more. An example of this would be stimming. This is a common self-stimulatory behavior to children with HFA, which is characterized by excessive flapping, repetition of behavior, tapping toes, or verbally. HFA children typically engage in these when excited, happy, anxious, or trapped in stressful situations. We may think that stimming can be controlled, yet for our HFA children, nervous stims are usually involuntary.

Some, however, can be hypersensitive; this means they cannot bear very loud noises or overwhelming situations. Most HFA children can't handle a certain temperature, staying in one place for a long period of time, tight clothing, or particular places. Nevertheless, our children have different sensory challenges, and understanding them is a significant step towards helping them feel more comfortable in any environment.

You can help your child overcome these sensory challenges by first being vigilant. Watch and observe closely how your child reacts to certain information around them. Take notes and write a daily journal if you can, listing down new discoveries on your child's sensory sensitivity to keep as a reference for the future. For instance, your child can be highly sensitive to bright lights or hot weather but can also yearn for constant touch and assurance when they arrive home from school. Most HFA children couldn't bear the constant flickering of lights, flapping curtains, constant mowing of lawns, dogs barking, water dripping, ticking of clocks, the list can go on. But also ensure you consider the various textures of food and materials, such as slippery and mushy, which can also cause stressors for your child.

Overcoming sensory challenges

Helping your child control these sensory differences depends on how they react to the information. If your child gets overwhelmed by situations easily, the best way to calm them down is to set up a quiet space where they can deescalate, or if the problem is with noise, have them try noise-canceling headphones that will help dampen the noise. If your child requires more stimulation, on the other hand, try handing them extra-stimulating toys such as squishy balls or slime. It could also help to arrange playtime outside and speak loudly to your child, especially if they are less responsive to sounds or noise.

Apart from those tools mentioned, there is also a technique where sensory differences can be treated through a therapy called sensory integration. It is performed only by occupational therapists and uses sensory activities that help our HFA child respond appropriately to sensory inputs. Activities can include brushing, swinging, bouncing, playing in the ball pit, and sometimes climbing, which stimulate sensory responses and improve their focus, behavior and lower their risks of anxiety attacks.

Preparing a Sensory Tool Kit

Once our HFA child reaches school age, we worry about plenty of things, like them coping with their new environment, making friends, and controlling sensory challenges. Now that we have observed and taken notes on sensory information that triggers our child's reception, we can prepare and build a repertoire of sensory tools for our child. Sensory tools are designed to promote sensory regulation, increase focus, and strengthen their readiness to learn. They support our children's various needs and stabilize their senses, helping them cope and regulate their sensory input.

You will want items that will calm your child by reducing stress or, conversely, sensory triggers and things that alert your child by providing sensory input. A key aspect of having a sensory toolkit is letting your child explore what you have and allow them to decide what is best when they are feeling overloaded. After your child has used a toy, ensure you explain why they have used it. To give an example, "That is a squeezy ball. You can use it when you feel like your body has too much energy and needs to calm down," providing an explanation builds association for your child, which can help reclaim their sensory regulation during times of distress.

3. Improving your Home Environment

Once you begin to address the task of understanding

your child's nonverbal cues and sensory differences, the next thing you should work on is improving your child's environment at home. Feeling a balance of comfort, safety, and happiness can create a better living situation for your children. Thus, it becomes one of the fundamental baselines of improving in other areas of their lives.

We should always have a designated space for our HFA children to decompress by the end of the day or whenever they feel overwhelmed. You can build their own corner that will serve as their "safe space" inside your home. Try creating or adding something that might interest your child, such as a play corner, bookshelves, music room, etc. This way, your child's mind can remain at work instead of an electronic device, which might even improve their thinking and communicating processes.

Avoid fluorescent lights as HFA children are usually sensitive to bright lights. Instead, give them the option to listen to music inside your home by giving them headphones or setting up a space where they can play music and play freely. However, If your child is sensitive to noise, consider listening to your music, podcasts, etc., through headphones instead of speakers to accommodate their stressors.

. . .

Cleaning Up

While setting a corner or space for your child is important, always remind them to keep these areas clean and tidy. It will help to designate a space where they can put back all their things after using them, a 'cleaning station' so to speak. This area of creating a home environment is probably one of the toughest.

When my son was nearly 8, I decided to buy him a paint set with different canvases to encourage his creative and artistic side. He loved this newfound activity for around six months. Every time, we would have to remind him to put his brushes back to their proper places, and he would gladly oblige. However, without reminding, he would often struggle to pack away properly, as he struggled with multi-step instructions at that time, a common trait of HFA. As a solution, we printed out reminders and checklists and stuck them clearly in his designated area. For this reason, a recommendation would be to buy a laminator to make your signs last. Eventually, he was able to tidy up after himself, with the odd occasion of him totally forgetting...but we're only human!

———

Given the three strategies above, our quest to better understand our HFA child is an ongoing process. I am aware that accommodating their needs is not as simple as it reads in this chapter. A lot of features throughout take trial and error. Your sensory toolkit, for instance, may take some time to figure out. Yet, if we put in extra time and effort to research, ask those thought-stimulating questions, and observe them beyond the words they are speaking, we can definitely break through these barriers and fully understand our HFA child.

4

USING YOUR CHILD'S INTERESTS TO
HELP THEM THRIVE

E ach of our HFA children has specific strengths and weaknesses, commonly being exceptionally honest, social cluelessness, and a very strong passion for a particular interest. We can choose to either let these bring us down or inspire us to hone our child's personality and abilities. As for me, I stand by the latter.

Despite the differences in the symptoms our HFA children manifest, the two main issues they always face are communication and social interaction. Parts of the previous chapters have touched on the measures you can take as a parent to help your child overcome these challenges. Yet, within this chapter, I will give you practical tips on how to harness these skills and turn their difficulties into their advantages, helping them not only to overcome but to thrive.

Knowing your Child's Strengths and Weaknesses

According to studies, 75 to 90% of people with ASD develop one or more special interests in their early life that tend to be maintained later in life. We can use these special interests to their advantage, but first, we should know their strengths and weaknesses.

Having years of experience teaching and caring for my HFA son, there is a range of abilities and strengths that most HFA children have in common, including quick memorization of things, preciseness and being detail-oriented, reliability in schedules and routines, punctuality, a high focus for a long period of time, a good sense of wonderment, perfectionism and being orderly, and many other traits that you may see in your child along the way.

Apart from the abilities that we see in our children, we can also use their difficulties to an advantage. For instance, their exceptional honesty, which can be challenging to live with at home, may help them be dependable at school. They can be modeled as an excellent example in their class for being completely honest, and we can teach them to use this honesty the right way. Moreover, this honesty may also help our child be exceedingly adherent to rules. You may find it helpful to create a list as your child grows, so you can keep track of their strengths and weaknesses, which will help you guide them in the direction that best suits them.

Harnessing interests to improve communication

We parents must learn which of these skills on our list our child is better at and use this to promote progress and growth. Remember that only they can use their strengths and interests to boost their learning and communication skills. You are there to guide them.

There are plenty of ways to improve our HFA child's communication skills using their unique interests. Once we have gathered a list of their strengths and have broken them down into the most appropriate field for our child, we can then assess the level of their skills so we can plot goals and plan for development. Setting goals is essential as it allows us to monitor their abilities and assess their improvement, and at the same time, it helps us provide and set supportive feedback to uplift them.

For instance, one of your HFA child's strengths is

memorizing things quickly and storing them in their memory for a long time. You can encourage your child to read more books that interest them and ask them questions or a quiz right after. Of course, make sure you do it in a fun way, for instance incorporating treats or rewards such as more screen time for correct answers. Utilizing their interests in this way boosts their self-esteem while improving their cognitive behaviors and intelligence. Having involvement in their interests will give them more confidence, especially if you are enthusiastic about their skills.

Another example would be if your child's unique skill were to have a high focus on a particular passion. When you see them so invested in doing something, like building legos and other nifty crafts, you can hone this skill by giving them more structures to make and play with and give them inspiration for more extensive and more intricate designs. In the beginning, you can encourage them to build things as a form of play, but as their skills develop and interest deepens, you can start giving them more complicated tasks, such as working as part of a team or beat their personal best and explain what they have made or done. Technology is great in today's age, as you can record them discussing their work and play it back to them. Ask them, "Do you think you explained yourself fully?" "Could you have talked about x, y, z?" This level of harnessing their interests and pursuing a dialogue will ensure they grow and progress in their communication abilities.

Telling your HFA child social stories that incorporate their special interest is also a helpful strategy. To give an example, if you notice that your child is fixated with planes or a particular aircraft, you can tell them how someone's love for airplanes turned them into a pilot. Have examples at the ready to illustrate the connection with one's passions and the possibility of making it a reality.

This can be made relevant to many instances, such as a love of Minecraft could lead to a job in video game design, or a passion for cars could be an avenue to work at the next F1 race. Although it may seem far-fetched, as a parent, you should aim to inspire and engage your child to want to progress their interest into a skill they could harness into a profession and excite them, which will encourage them to talk about it. Most HFA children will not struggle to talk about their passions (usually they can go on and on!); however, adding complexity to their vocabulary and sentence structure will come if you encourage purposeful discussions.

. . .

Praise

Utilizing praise is of the utmost importance when honing their interests and passions to improve their communication skills. If they have done something well, tell them, but more significantly, ask them how they feel. Good, great, proud? Asking these key questions while giving praise gives meaning to the words you speak and stimulates their understanding of emotions. It will soon become part of their dialogue, which they can tap into on all occasions if done regularly.

The Importance of Play

Never underestimate the importance of play, both physical and pretend. Physical play is a pretty vital part of anyone's childhood because it gives children the opportunity to socialize with others, build intuitive social skills, and engage in more exercise and motor skills development. Growing up, a child needs to be active in physical activities that can help improve their overall well-being.

For your HFA child, physical play means more than exercise; it also means they have the opportunity to be exposed to social interaction and face-to-face communication with children of their age. Now, I understand that these may be two challenging factors for them to deal with, but we should encourage them to interact with others, not force them, and accept the times when they wish to play on their own. A good method to motivate them to play is to intertwine their special skills/interests into playtime.

Pretend Play

Aside from physical play, we can also encourage or set up our HFA child with pretend plays. These types of play are typically used on ages two and above, which enhances their development. There are two kinds of pretend play, **in vivo** and **in vitro**. An in vivo pretend play allows your child to use only themselves while acting, without props. This pretense can include various scenarios and activities where they pretend to be different characters.

In vitro pretend play, on the other hand, allows children to use props such as dolls, puppets, and other objects and act for them instead of for themselves. The object then becomes a character that your child creates. For example, your child uses a doll, names her Barbara, and assigns characteristics different from their own. This can help increase their creativity level and even encourage interaction.

. . .

I once taught a young boy in Grade Prep who was parallel playing with a young girl. This means that they are playing side by side without influencing each other's behavior. HFA children usually love playing alone but often get interested in what another child is doing. The young girl was giving her doll a cup of tea and a cookie which the young boy thought was absolutely ridiculous, as it was a stuffed doll which, of course, could not eat or drink. At first, he felt that she was stupid because he could only think literally. Once encouraged to communicate his feelings, it led to discussion and interaction, albeit not very much, but it was a small win in improving his communication.

Pretend play is vital in helping your child develop skills for interaction, communication, and building social relationships. It can also help your child feel empathy for other people that they play roles in.

Special interest or obsessive-compulsive disorder?

As excellent as it is to utilize your child's interests, you must be conscious of their interests, as using them to their advantage can be great for enhancing skills. However, that passion they have could be obsessive-compulsive disorder. Be aware that OCD is different from Obsessive-Compulsive Personality Disorder (OCPD), which is a mental disorder. These people are characterized by their need for control and perfectionism, whereas OCD is defined by obsessions and compulsions, which interfere with daily life and do not go away. For example, a child may have an obsession with having things in a particular way. Their compulsions are to check, count, order, wash or touch things in a repetitive or ritual-like way to counteract the distress and anxiety produced from the obsessive thoughts. If you can see these traits in your child, the best option is to seek therapy, such as CBT.

Tools to improve social interaction

Social interaction Vs. the proper social response is often dependent on the context of the situation, which is why our HFA children frequently misconstrue the social response. To give an example, when parents see friends and family, we shake hands, hug and kiss our loved ones, although, for our HFA children, it can be hard to gauge how long a hug should last or precisely where a kiss should be placed. This lack of social awareness can be down to many factors, such as sensory distraction, memory dysfunction, or affective processing. With a bit of guidance, you can encourage the correct behaviors; although it is imperative to comprehend that these skills need to be explicitly taught to our HFA children, it is not something that comes naturally to them. For this reason, there are numerous therapies you can engage with, such as social integration therapy and many, if not all of the therapies outlined in chapter 2. If you are not indulging in therapy for social interaction, then there are many tips that will help your child formulate social awareness, which you can do at home.

A good starting place is to remind your child of the appropriate and positive behaviors they should exhibit. This is particularly pertinent when you are in public spaces such as the supermarket or shopping mall, as our children with HFA are prone to blurt out something inappropriate and often loud. When these occasions pop up, take them aside and jog their memory on what it means to show others our positive behavior.

Ensure you cue them with what to do, as opposed to what *not* to do, "Remember not to shout out naughty or rude words when we are in the store." Vs. "Remember, we like to show people that we have positive behavior and act in a way that is polite and friendly." Limiting the use of negative language, such as 'no, don't and stop' is an intuitive parenting tool to rewire our children's brains for positivity. This does not mean cutting these words out of your vocabulary, although I recommend you cut down to make your children listen better. By using positive language, you enable your child to fully grasp what you are asking, as simply saying "Don't shout" does not give them direction in what they *can* do. It also gives power to the word no when it is used.

Encouraging turn-taking is another great way to build on social skills. Playing board games, video games, outdoor games, and particularly sharing possessions such as crayons, pens or toys, are all vital moments for you to promote how to take turns, even when it can be frustrating for your child. Show your child how to sit quietly and wait whilst others participate and take their turn.

Again, you may use your child's interests to join groups, societies, or clubs related to their area of interest. Be cautious of the groups they go to, or more specifically, the other children involved, as it is very common for HFA children to be led astray, especially in their pre-teen years. A helpful tip is to liaise with the support staff or group leaders and ask them which children are good role models for your child to follow. Providing your child with good examples that they can observe is important as it shows them how to behave.

. . .

Utilizing reflection is an integral part of growing up; even into adulthood, we are encouraged to look back and reflect on our actions and behaviors to improve for the next time. In any situation that arises, that isn't handled with the best social response, help your child reflect on what they could have done better and explain why. Create your own social stories based on real-life events that require guidance.

Utilizing these opportunities will develop their understanding. It will take time, and you may have to go over the same social story numerous times, yet you must persevere and be explicit. When explaining why an action is inappropriate, the explanation may have to come in several ways worded differently to make your child understand. I taught a young girl who was 5 and took off her clothes when she was excited. After speaking with her parents, I found out that she took her uniform off when she arrived home from school as it was her happy place, and that was her way of expressing her excitement. When in school, support staff and I had to explain that she should not expose her private parts in public (and the reason why) because they are her private parts that people should not be able to see. The bottom line, regardless of the scenario, be explicit.

The battle with self-esteem

It must be made clear that irrespective of promoting their interests and harnessing their communication and social skills, low self-esteem is more common for our children with HFA, which can lead to isolation and depression. Self-esteem is defined by our beliefs and feelings we have about ourselves. It is what influences our attitude, motivations, and behaviors; therefore, it is essential that we foster healthy self-esteem in our youngsters.

Cultivating high self-esteem using the tools discussed in this chapter will make your child feel good about themselves, making it easier for them to handle conflicts and frustrations. There are several signs to look out for when assessing low self-esteem: your child speaking negatively about themselves on a regular basis, with comments such as "I will never be able to do this" or a resistance to trying new things and giving up easily. My son was overly critical about himself when he was age 10/11, as he became disappointed in himself very quickly when he lost a game of chess or any game he was good at, which is another telltale sign of low esteem.

. . .

If you spot these signs, then there are a number of ways you can help improve their low esteem. Firstly, be a role model. If you are often pessimistic or excessively harsh on yourself, then your child may mirror behavior. Secondly, you must believe in your child and have empathy for them, not sympathy. Tuning into their special gifts with compassion and genuine interest will bring out their true selves, which is why you must be affectionate with your actions and your words.

Praise as mentioned is also essential in boosting self-esteem, so parents should be enthusiastic but, most importantly, honest. As they get older, children can tell if you are false, so do not overload them with unnecessary praise. To raise esteem, you should stress the effort they are making even before they have reached a goal to uplift them during working progress and empower them to be themselves by loving them for who they are irrespective of their progress.

Another major factor for deterring low self-esteem for my son was entering constructive experiences rather than competitions as they encourage cooperation instead of the urge to win. This works particularly well if they have younger siblings; you can invite them to build something together or read together, which can do wonders to help both children learn.

. . .

Lastly, children with HFA are expert copycats, which is why you must be careful what you say around them as they may go declaring something to their class that they probably shouldn't!

————

Getting to know your child is part and partial of being a parent, although understanding a HFA child comes with an extra set of challenges that require a lot more of our time and energy to handle. Harnessing their interests for increased communication and utilizing social stories for improved social interaction are useful and highly recommended, although, at the end of a long day, it is you that manifests positive change as you are their most trusted mentor. Provided you are trying, even if it is just one of these strategies mentioned, you are striving for your child to do better, which means you are positive parenting. Take pride in that. You are doing your best.

Yet, I'm sure you are thinking, there are times when it just doesn't work! There will be times when you struggle to achieve the goals you set or maintain positive behaviors, which is where boundary-setting becomes essential.

5

OVERCOMING THE BATTLE WITH BOUNDARIES

Excess of anything is bad. No one can exist without boundaries to guide them through life, and children are no exception. Every child learns how to recognize boundaries from their parents. This means parents are solely responsible for setting boundaries and determining what is right and wrong for their children.

One prominent aspect of setting boundaries we will talk about in this chapter is limiting screen time for your HFA child.

Setting Boundaries

Children with HFA often have difficulty coping with many things in life, especially when it comes to boundaries. So when you ask your child to do something, and they don't do it, do you let it go? Or do you feel that what you want them to do is impossible?

Discipline is one of the most important things involved in raising a child. Every child needs discipline irrespective of their mental or physical needs. This can be especially difficult for parents with HFA children. However, every HFA child needs rules, regulations, and guidelines as it will help them live better and grow into responsible adults.

The first step in setting boundaries for your HFA child is knowing the line between being too harsh and spoiling them. This is probably the most challenging aspect of disciplining a child on the autism spectrum. HFA children require clear rules and regulations that will guide their behavior and give them an idea of their expectations.

Without any boundaries, HFA children end up behaving in ways that are not acceptable to societal standards or your own. It is not uncommon for people to see HFA children as oppositional, resistant, and non-compliant.

The reality for children on the autism spectrum without any rules and boundaries guiding their behavior is likely to lead them not knowing how to behave and understand what is expected of them. This can make them more anxious, irritable, and more likely to behave in unacceptable ways. So the question we must address is, how do you set clear boundaries for your HFA child without being too hard on them and without spoiling them?

Take advantage of your child's debating skills

The first step in setting boundaries for your child is negotiating with them. Your child already knows what they want, and you know what you expect of your child. It is left for you to negotiate how to influence your child to behave correctly. Unlike other children, your child requires special attention when it comes to setting boundaries. Speak with your child about what disturbs them. For instance, if they don't like eating asparagus, you can agree that they will eat every other vegetable on the plate apart from asparagus. Or if they always get anxious because of how you are dressing them, you can speak to them and find out how they like to be dressed. My son hated wearing blue. Once we discovered this (which took a number of months!), it was a simple process of elimination that made the morning dress routine a thousand times easier. With time you can come to learn about those things they find offensive.

Another way to utilize their debating skills is to give them choices with no option to say no. For instance, instead of asking your child would you like to go shopping today? You can ask, when will you want to go shopping; Tuesday or Wednesday? By taking advantage of your child's debating skills, you include them in the decision-making process, giving them a sense of independence. Many parents fear that they will spoil their child by negotiating what they want. However, negotiating with your child about the boundaries they need to keep or instructions they need to abide by, tells them that their feelings are important.

Avoid surprises

If there is one thing a vast majority of HFA children hate, it is surprises. Any changes to their daily routine or interruptions to their usual regime should be avoided unless absolutely necessary. Of course, there will be times when your child's routine will be interrupted, but this is where you can take advantage of your child's negotiating skills. Speak to them about the change and tell them about any available alternate options.

When your child is faced with change, there is a strong likelihood of a tantrum or a meltdown. So it is essential not to get annoyed when they disagree with the available alternatives. They might even call you "stupid" and blame you for the surprise change in their routine. In such situations, you must remain calm and see things from a clear mind. Easier said than done, especially if you are late for an appointment! Yet as a parent of a HFA child reading this book, today is the day you must endeavor to maintain and sustain a sense of calm in all areas of life.

Ensure boundaries are collaborated with you and your partner - show a united front

Both parents or guardians must make sure that they present a united front on all boundaries and rules. You must encourage and work together to come up with strategies that will work for everyone. Your child should receive the same treatment for unwanted behaviors from both parents. Together you should agree on getting your child to follow the rules and boundaries all three parties agreed to follow by discussing with your child, no matter how old they are.

Explain to your child that a boundary is in place for several reasons, such as it "Doing XYZ keeps you safe; therefore you must follow this rule, so you don't get hurt." At a young age, children are responsive to explicit teaching, be clear and ensure you always explain "why" they should or should not be doing something.

Encourage reflection

The way you react to your child's tantrums or misbehavior should aim to have your child reflect on their decisions and behaviors. The goal is always to be empathetic, soothing, and respectful. You should try to meet your child's inflexibility with flexibility. For example, if they pull their foot away while you are trying their shoe, and they say, "You are hurting my foot, stupid." Rather than replying with "Stop talking to me that way," you can take your time and respond with, "Maybe your foot is a little sensitive." Before you continue tying her shoe, you can ask them how tight they want their shoe to be. Sometime later, once they are completely calm, you can discuss why they yelled and called you stupid. This way you can help them reflect on why they've been so unnecessarily unfair to you.

The more you help recognize this pattern of behavior, the more they can learn to be considerate towards you, instead of yelling at you. Embracing reflection will enable you to be more empathetic and also logical when evaluating a scenario.

A child I taught in Grade 4 called me an idiot when

I asked him about his homework on a Monday morning. Instead of reacting instantly and saying, "Don't speak to your teacher like that!" I responded with, "Why am I an idiot? I know I am not perfect, but I think that is a little insensitive to my feelings." I was explicit with the "why" I reacted in that way to instigate the child's meaningful reflection. My calm reply to him took a lot of work on my part because it can be extremely difficult to be calm in that kind of situation. Yet when it comes to your HFA child, you must endeavor to be controlled, as an erratic parent equals an erratic child.

Reward when boundaries are kept

The best way to get your child to do what you both agreed to is to reward them when they keep to a boundary. Everyone likes to be rewarded for doing something well, and this is the same for your HFA child. When your child gets a reward such as praise for behaving a certain way, it triggers a relationship between good behavior and praise, which reinforces desirable behaviors. For instance, you can say, "I'm really proud of you for ending your screen time on time this evening because that shows me you are a good listener." This praise is clear and concise, which fully reinforces the desired behavior. The delivery of recognition and praise should be consistent and systematic. The larger the accomplishment, the bigger the praise, which coincides with the timing of your words. Ensure to deliver praise immediately after the desired behavior as the reward is most powerful when given straight after the good behavior was shown.

Consequences of not keeping a boundary

In the same way we use rewards for good behavior, consequences are the answer to unfavorable behaviors. The consequences of not adhering to a set boundary should have a relevant consequence that is directly linked to the behavior. For instance, if your child is repeatedly hitting one of their toys on the ground, you can take away some or all of their toys as a consequence.

Always ensure that the consequence for your child's failure to keep a boundary is linked to something they value. For instance, withdrawing attention away from a HFA child might seem like a punishment to some children. However, for a child who prefers to be alone, your lack of attention might be more of a benefit than punishment. A more appropriate punishment for such a child might be taking away a favorite video game for some time.

After your child has faced the consequence of their

behavior, you can work with them to develop a better behavior as a replacement. For example, if your child is trying to get your attention by speaking too loudly, both of you can work on coming up with a better way of getting your attention, such as a light tap on your shoulder or a signal you both agree upon.

The goal is to always work with your child to develop a replacement behavior for an inappropriate one. With time your child can learn to associate your positive response to the replacement behavior and gradually do away with the bad behavior.

Be consistent

As previously mentioned, HFA children are generally not comfortable with change. A HFA child needs a stable environment with constant rules and expectations to thrive. It is wise to maintain a morning routine or adhere to dinner manners as an everyday endeavor as a family. It is crucial to let your child know that certain things are expected of them at certain times, and they must keep to it. Be conscious of times or scenarios when you have to remind your child of the boundaries they need to keep. When you are reminding them, ensure that you are clear, realistic, and affirmative.

With time, your HFA child can learn to predict

what will happen if they fail to keep a boundary. This will help them live in an environment where they understand barriers and right from wrong. As a child, they will always want to push beyond these boundaries, but it is up to you to ensure they keep to the standards put in place.

Although it is sometimes inevitable to have a change in routine, for example, the library might be closed for redecorating, or the park is closed for an event. As parents, you need to know your limits. If something is inaccessible, for instance, they cannot go swimming; you have to decide upon a decision that will make your life easier. Do not beat yourself up or feel you are giving in if you have to compromise with your set boundary for that particular occasion. There will be days when some things are out of your control. As a repercussion, you might have to watch their favorite movie for the afternoon, even if they have seen it 100 times!

Limiting screen time

HFA children often have difficulty understanding the world around them. It can take just a little trigger for them to become hypo/hyperactive. Our HFA children are prone to repeating certain behaviors, which makes it hard for them to interact with others. For this Reason, digital devices are what they turn to when they need to escape the world around them. It provides them with predictable outcomes which can calm them down when they are distressed and help them perform in line with their own pace. It is also an easy option for parents when in public, especially dining out, which many HFA children are not big fans! Do not be ashamed if you are quick to hand over the device on occasions like these, as parents sometimes need some reprieve too! As for my son, it was a miracle for him to be sitting in a restaurant, so I get it.

According to research, HFA children spend a considerable amount of time on digital devices than other children. This is because these devices provide them with an environment where they can predict what will happen. While digital devices can be helpful for your HFA child, they can also be unhealthy if their use is not regulated.

Regulating your child's screen time might probably be the most challenging thing you will do when it comes to creating boundaries. A digital device is the only place they have complete control of what is happening around them. However, you must monitor your child's screen time for their benefit and yours. Before we talk about how you can do that, let's talk about *why* you should.

. . .

Effect of excessive screen time on your HFA child:

- **Too much screen time can stunt social development.**

HFA children experience difficulty in dealing with social interactions and expressing themselves. While screen time provides your child with a controlled environment, it also means they are missing out on life interactions with their peers. This, in turn, makes it even more difficult to develop the necessary skills needed for social interaction. Too much screen time is also associated with a delay in language learning in HFA children.

- **It's a stimulant for children with HFA and leads to a release of dopamine.**

Digital devices produce numerous stimuli, which can be too much for a HFA child. This can worsen their behavior by making them more anxious and irritated.

Too much screen time has the same effect as stress hormones on your child. Digital screens produce electromagnetic fields (EMF), which is especially harmful to most HFA children because they are extremely sensitive to them. EMF stimulates the release of dopamine, a hormone that is responsible for excitement. This usually makes your child more anxious and irritable.

According to research, screen time is often associated with obsessive-compulsive disorders (OCD), since HFA children are more prone to be affected by obsessive-compulsive disorders and social anxiety, more screen time only serves to increase OCD.

● **Affects sleep patterns.**

Studies show that screen time affects sleep patterns. It is especially true for HFA children who suffer from a poor bedtime routine. Screen-time suppresses melatonin which is a natural sleep hormone that is responsible for regulating the body's clock. This interrupts sleep rhythm and can lead to insomnia and other sleep disorders, but most importantly, getting them to sleep at the beginning of the night!

Melatonin is also responsible for regulating the body's immune system, and lack of sleep only leads to inflammation of the nervous system. The body responds to lack of sleep by releasing stress hormones which puts the body in a constant state of hyperactivity. This makes your child hyperactive and highly irritable, which makes it difficult for them to function well and, of course, go to sleep!

● **Unsafe content.**

The internet is filled with numerous unsafe content. It is your job as a parent to keep your child protected from any content that will harm their physical and mental health. There are applications capable of tracking what your child can do on a device. It is highly recommended that you employ them to help monitor and regulate the things your child can access.

The difference between Active screen time (engaged in an app) VS passive (watch a video)

According to psychologists, we have two ways of using technology – active and passive screen time.

During active screen time, we are actively learning, and using our minds. For your child, active screen time could mean reading something online or even playing an interactive game that requires active use of the mind or video chatting with a friend. Passive screen time, on the other hand, involves watching a movie or film or scrolling absent-mindedly through the internet.

As you already guessed, active screen time is the more productive of the two, and your child should spend more time actively using a screen.

Children use their computers for schoolwork in this day and age, meaning they may be spending more time than you may deem appropriate looking at a screen. Irrespective of what your child uses their device for, your job as their parent is to make sure they spend more time doing something productive, rather than just scrolling on social media or Netflix. You are in the best position to identify when your child needs some time away from their screen. Be observant if their behavior becomes erratic or they appear tired after long periods using a screen. Even as adults looking at a screen for too many hours can be exhausting; the same applies to our children.

Be wary if your child finds it hard to focus on their studies or spend more time on their phone instead of building in-person relationships with friends and family. These are both fundamental reasons why you should be limiting screen time.

Methods to limit screen time
• Structure time zones

You can regulate screen time by dedicating a certain amount of time for screen time and sticking to it. The maximum amount of time for using all digital devices should be 3-4 hours per day. You can set out times during the day when they can have access to a digital device. The best time is generally between 3-6 pm before dinner and after school.

Implementing this regime means that your child sits and eats dinner without distraction and can then decompress after dinner in time for bedtime. Ensure that your child keeps away from a screen a minimum of 30 minutes before going to bed to allow time to unwind, ready for sleep.

Aim to be a role model for your child by not using your screen at the dinner table (phone, tablet, etc.). This way, you are setting an example and reinforcing good behaviors. As a result, not using a screen while eating should come as natural to them.

Another useful tip when setting effective boundaries is to always give a 10-minute heads up before the end of the screen time. You can set timers to track the time spent, which provides visual cues for your child and gives your child clear guidance for when the screen time will be over. I always made all my children say how long they had left back to me, just so it was abundantly clear that they knew.

- **Turn off their phone service**

This is one of the best ways of regulating screen time for your child. It limits what they can do on a device. So during long journeys, they are left with magazines and books to read, instead of the internet and games. Almost everything interesting a child can do in today's society is with a device and through the internet. From social media to gaming, there are limitless things a child can do with the internet. For this reason, many children find their digital devices boring when there is no phone service. This means if you truly want to get your child to abandon their device, turning off their phone service is the best way to go about it for certain scenarios.

• No electronics in the bedroom

This is a major rule that all parents should follow if they want their child to sleep better. There's no reason why your HFA child should have electronics in their bedroom. Electronic devices such as TV, iPad, phones shouldn't be left in the same room with your child. Otherwise, you are only encouraging them to do what they want when they are supposed to be sleeping. At first, it will be a challenge to remove devices from their bedroom, but once their room is digitally free, not only can you easily track their amount of screen time, but you will see an improvement in their sleep routine.

• Read together

Ridding devices from their bedroom is one strategy that should be replaced with reading. This gives you a chance to nurture a bedtime routine that involves story-telling and book reading which will develop their love of reading, literacy skills, and imagination. According to studies, beginning to read with your child during their formative age helps them develop language and increase their vocabulary as they interact and bond with you. This also Builds their trust in you. Apart from the fact that reading before bedtime keeps them away from a screen, it can also be a fun activity that you and your HFA child will nurture together and look forward to. If reading a book isn't an appealing option, Storytime.online has a comprehensive library of books read aloud, which you could watch together.

• Avoid negotiating

The one thing you should not do when it comes to screen time for your HFA Child is allowing negotiating for more screen time. Although screen time can be used as a reward for good behaviors or doing house chores, you must be consistent with your boundaries. It is not advisable to let your child negotiate an increased screen time. This, of course, is exceptionally challenging, especially if your child is prone to tantrums. Yet, if you allow them to do so, it will only be a slippery slope that gives them more opportunity to push the boundaries in place.

There are numerous documented effects of excessive screen time and digital devices on children. The issues that arise due to excessive screen time for HFA children are a cause for concern. Therefore, as a parent, you should try as much as possible to regulate the screen time for your HFA child. However, your HFA child is not like other children, and it can be especially difficult to get the right balance between not spoiling and disciplining them. Your HFA child, like any other child, will try to push the boundaries you set. There are times when they will scream, threaten you, and say things like "I hate you." But remember, this is normal for any child, and it should be expected from all children at some stage in their childhood. Screaming and saying damming things is their way of reacting to their needs. Depending on the boundary you have set, especially if it is screen time, it will take a while for your child to accept it, yet with sincere perseverance from you as a parent or guardian, they will learn to respect the rules you have put in place.

With time, your child will push less and scream less as they move towards accepting the boundary. The journey toward accepting setting boundaries can be difficult. As a parent, you have to know when to pick your battles. When your child has a tough time accepting a boundary, you may have to make a compromise or exception. Evaluate if the act is causing harm and analyze whether putting your foot down will cause more damage than good. For instance, I taught a boy in grade 6 obsessed with trains. He had mountains of tickets, maps, timetables, pamphlets, brochures that were overflowing his family home, so much so, his mum and dad had to start putting boxes in the attic! On this new journey, you will have to accept that you will be making accommodations that aren't ideal at times to make your child happy.

. . .

There is a fine line between being too lenient and spoiling your child. As a parent who wants the best for your child, you have to discipline them using the proper methods so they grow up to become responsible adults. The only way you can achieve this is by setting boundaries. If you are worried about being too harsh on your child, discuss with them and agree on boundaries together. The majority of children know that they shouldn't be on a device for hours on end, so discussing boundaries together might not be as challenging as you think. Listening to what your child has to say doesn't mean you are spoiling them; it only means you care and respect your child enough to listen to what they have to say. If you want to make sure your child maintains all the boundaries you both agreed to, then you have to be consistent with all the consequences attached to the failure to keep them.

The amount of screen time your child should have is a major boundary you will need to decide as a parent. Always make sure there is a healthy balance between the amount of time your child spends on their screen and in-person social interactions. Depending on your child's age, you can discuss with your child's doctor the best amount of passive screen time suitable for your child.

————

With consistent boundaries, they can learn to behave in ways that will bring rewards instead of consequences. Setting and maintaining boundaries determines your child's behaviors and are especially important when sustaining house routines, rules, and guidelines. However, for children to adhere to set boundaries, it is to be expected that there will be tantrums and possibly meltdowns on the journey that gets you there. In the next chapter, I'll be talking about the secrets to managing those difficult times.

6

THE SECRETS TO MANAGING THOSE DIFFICULT TIMES

One of the most challenging things for parents with HFA children is knowing what to do when the child goes through an emotional, mental breakdown, or a meltdown. Your child, just like any other child, is going to go through difficult times both emotionally and mentally. It's your job as a parent to help them go through it.

Many parents of HFA children go through hard times dealing with a meltdown episode, especially if you are new to their diagnosis. You start doubting yourself because you cannot calm your child or control their actions during a meltdown: Can I do this? Am I fit to be their parent?

It can be grueling when you do not understand why your child reacts in a certain way or is emotionally unstable with a particular stressor. What do you do when they become overwhelmed with everything that's happening? How can you deal with your child when they are throwing a tantrum or having a meltdown. This chapter is all about helping you answer these questions, but most importantly, it will teach you how to help your child whenever they are going through a tough time.

Most parents with HFA children find it hard to tell the difference between when they are having a meltdown and when they have a temper tantrum. Knowing the difference between the two helps you in coming up with an appropriate solution.

The difference between a tantrum and a meltdown

A child can throw a **tantrum** when:

- They are frustrated for not getting what they want
- They not able to do what they like
- They are not able to communicate effectively

The tantrum usually comes to an end when the child is comforted by a parent, given what they want or ignored. As a result, they stop the tantrum by themselves. The child is often in total control of their actions when throwing a tantrum. They can even adjust the level of tempers depending on the kind of response they are getting. In other words, the child can easily control their emotions and behavior.

A **meltdown**, on the other hand, is an intense reaction due to sensory overload. Autistic children experience a breakdown when their senses are overloaded, and they cannot express themselves properly. Their response can include screaming, crying, and other physical reactions such as hitting, biting, and so on.

A meltdown might look like a tantrum; however, they have a different purpose. A child usually throws a tantrum to get what they want. On the other hand, a meltdown has no outcome or goal attached and is out of the child's control.

Although **symptoms** of meltdowns vary for every child, it may include any of the following:

- It begins with pre-meltdown symptoms known as rumblings. These can be physical behaviors or verbal signs that signal an incoming meltdown.
- Stimming may also be an initial symptom: this is also known as self-stimulatory

behavior. It is a usual or repetitive noise or body movement. It might include - finger and hand mannerisms or body movement, or other repetitive behaviors: for instance, finger-flicking, rocking back and forth while sitting, closing and opening doors, or flicking switches.

- It can happen in the presence of people or when no one is around.
- It lasts longer than tantrums.
- Telling the difference between a tantrum and a meltdown is the key to helping your child overcome their difficult situation.

How to deal with a tantrum

Although the strategies involved in dealing with a tantrum and a meltdown are similar, there are many differences in dealing with them. Procedures involved in dealing with a tantrum include:

1. Keep calm

The first thing many parents do when their autistic child is throwing a tantrum is to get angry, probably because they're overwhelmed, but doing so will only prolong your child's tantrum. Always try as much as possible to keep calm before dealing with your child's tantrums. Be sure to remember that: they are children, and throwing tantrums is part of what they do; they can't help themselves sometimes; tantrums might be a way of them seeking attention. When you realize these things, you can learn to keep calm no matter the situation and handle your child's tantrums with a clear mind.

2. **Do not give in**

The quickest way to stop your child's tantrum is to give them what they want. There is no shame in this, as a parent, you will have to pick your battles, and there will be situations where giving them something, in particular, will help soothe a process, such as being in the doctors or a situation in which your child isn't a fan. However, this is not the best option in the long run. Be cautious when giving your child what they are asking for on a regular basis, as it will only reinforce their bad behavior and show acceptance to tantrums.

3. **Acknowledge your child's emotions**

This is usually the first step in dealing with a tantrum. It simply involves showing your child that you understand and care about what they are saying. This is key when overcoming a tantrum and is crucial when dealing with a meltdown, so we'll discuss this further later in this chapter.

. . .

Explain Why Good Behavior is Important

Describe why their negative behavior isn't a good way to respond to the reason. Explain in simple words: "it is undesirable because..." make sure your child understands your reasoning. Once you are sure they know, you can describe what you want them to do instead: a replacement behavior as discussed in Chapter 5. For instance, if your child is screaming because they do not like a piece of food on their plate, you can explain why such behavior is wrong then come up with a strategy to overcome such a situation. For example, you could use a silicone plate divider that enables food to be separated. Therefore, if there is a new food on their plate, it will not touch the other foods and could decrease the likelihood of unwanted behaviors. Similarly, you could come up with a signal that illustrates when your child isn't happy with something new, such as a head shake or a hand gesture (which you can make fun!) to replace the unwanted screaming. There will be a considerable amount of trial and error on your behalf, although you will have to put the effort in to set up sufficient boundaries.

After coming up with a replacement behavior, you need to explain to your child why following the replacement behavior is important. Just like you did for the bad behavior, explain in simple words why the new behavior is better and should be used at all times. This is just as important as explaining why a behavior isn't acceptable, especially if your child is the inquisitive type who likes asking for reasons why they should behave in a certain way.

Deliver consequences

As a parent, you should understand that consequences are not equal to punishment. In the previous chapter, we talked about consequences as a result of bad behaviors. Just as with everything in life, there are consequences for every action. Yet remember, the consequence is to *teach* and *not* to punish.

There are rewards for good behaviors; likewise, there are also consequences for unfavorable behaviors. This is what you should discuss with your child. Both of you should agree on consequences for bad behaviors; this way, they know what to expect for every misbehavior. Explain the essence of cause and effect. For instance, anytime you scream to get my attention instead of calling or tapping me softly on my shoulder, I'm going to reduce your free time.

An imperative thing to understand is that consequences should be tangible, not just some imaginary and ambiguous action. It should be directly related to the cause. Similarly, if your child doesn't enjoy watching TV, there is no use taking TV time away. Ensure the consequence is something your child would miss. It must also be related to the action in both magnitude and size – the smaller the misbehavior, the smaller the consequence.

Consequences shouldn't come days or weeks after the action; they should happen immediately after the incident. This way, you can reinforce the good behavior and your child can instantly connect the consequence to their bad behaviors. Additionally, always make sure you follow through for every consequence; otherwise, your child will want to push through those boundaries as mentioned in the previous chapter: Consistency is critical.

Sometimes you may have to switch or change the consequence of an action if your strategy isn't working. It is only normal that as your child grows, they may outgrow certain consequences or become accustomed to the consequence, which inevitably diminishes the effect. The learning process never stops! Keep reinventing new ways and consequences that will keep your child in line and in check because there is no doubt your child will outgrow some consequences. With time, your confidence and abilities to make sure your child keeps to a boundary by using appropriate consequences will develop and grow.

When my son was a preteen, I often said that I would call the police if he continued to disrespect property. But I never did! I feel that I should have done, so he would have understood my consequences were concrete. If I could go back, I wouldn't have said that as it showed my son that I wasn't affirmative with my set consequences.

How to Deal with a meltdown
Validate their feelings to reassure them – use empathy

This is the first step in dealing with any HFA child going through a difficult time. Validate your child's feelings by showing interest and empathy. When your child is going through a tough time, like during a meltdown - this is not the right time to say, "You are acting like a child." Understand that your child is not in control of their actions which at first can be challenging, although it is the main step in gaining their trust and providing the reassurance they need. Even if their reaction is probably out of scale, try not to dismiss their feelings and struggles, small or large.

. . .

Ensure to get your child's attention by calling their name softly during a meltdown. When you have their attention, you can begin to speak to them in an even tone. Explain to them that you understand what they are going through and you want to help them in whatever way you can. When you validate and reorganize their feelings, you make them feel loved and understood. Recognizing their feelings doesn't mean you support their bad actions or behavior. It only shows you that you understand and see things from their perspective.

The following phrases are examples of ways you can validate your child's feelings:

"that must have hurt..."
"I know it's hard..."
"It's difficult when you don't do as well as you wanted to..."
"Losing doesn't feel good..."
"We all feel bad when..."
"I can see you are feeling..."
"that can be very annoying..."
"I feel the same way to when..."
"I bet you're not happy because..."
"I know what you mean..."

Using comments and phrases such as these in uncertain times shows your child empathy. You are not only making your child feel understood; you are also teaching them how to regulate and manage their feelings better by becoming more emotionally aware.

Ask, "How can I help you? "

"How can I help you "is a phrase that almost every human likes to hear. As an adult, hearing that phrase provides comfort even if it doesn't solve our problems. This is also the same for our children. You can say it in almost any difficult situation your child is going through. You can say it when they're frustrated, sad, angry, anxious, or having difficulty with homework. Asking if your child needs help coupled with showing empathy is a recipe for validation.

So instead of saying things like" I don't understand why you are acting like this," when they are going through a meltdown, you can simply say, "How can I help you? "You can also say this in moments when they are angry or throwing a tantrum. Instead of saying, "Act your age," say, "How can I help you." Reacting according to your first emotion will only worsen things: this is a common mistake parents make. Take a deep breath and remember that your child isn't trying to make your life miserable and that they need your help. You can only help them by analyzing the situation calmly. Saying "How can I help you" helps in providing support and reassurance for any particular situation.

Don't be surprised if your child's answer to your question is "you can't so leave me alone," or in my son's case when he was 12 – "You can help me by leaving me alone." When your child matures and enters their preteen years, the truth is you're more likely to get an unfavorable answer than a favorable one. If your child's response to your question is for you to leave them alone, then do so. Sometimes we need to be on our own to figure things out, which can be the same for your child.

It is common for parents to overcomplicate things sometimes, so providing they are safe and free from stressors, it's best to leave them alone when they want to be left alone. The goal is to validate their feelings to diffuse the situation and show your child that you are always available when they need it.

Remain calm

Similar to dealing with a tantrum, remaining calm is essential. When it comes to taking care of HFA children, remaining calm is a must if you want to help end a meltdown. Being angry or frustrated will only add fire to your child's behavior. You can't achieve the change or the result you want by showing erratic behaviors. The only result you can achieve by being erratic during meltdowns is a misunderstood child and a frustrated adult. No matter how heated and difficult the situation might be, remaining calm will limit your child's reactions and soothe them during meltdowns. This is far from easy, it will take time and practice, but it is achievable.

See Behavior as Communication and Address the Why

After every tantrum or meltdown, when your child is calm, is the time where you and your child have the chance to learn how to deal with situations better for the future. In other words, it allows you to address the "why" behind the behavior. Your child doesn't exist to torture you with their bad behaviors. If they could behave better or do better, they would. To help support your child, you need to identify why your child is behaving the way they do and develop strategies to help your child overcome their adversity. You can't rely on punishment and fear to overcome the reason. To change a behavior, address the reason behind it.

Only once they have de-escalated after a meltdown should you address your child and find out why they were behaving uncontrollably. More often than not, it won't be a simple conversation, although persevere and try to understand why your child acted out. This may take some investigatory skills on your behalf, as some children will not be able to describe why they are acting or feeling in an overt way. There is no right or wrong method to underpinning your child's behaviors, although being vigilant and conscientious in scenarios you think may be an issue is a good starting place to highlight things you could avoid in the future.

One day, a young girl who attended an autism group with my son was distraught when she arrived at the center. Her parents were baffled as to the reasoning for it. It took them days and hours of tears to realize that the route they drove to the center had roadworks with temporary traffic lights, which the little girl could not handle and was a big trigger for her.

How to prevent meltdowns?

For parents, dealing with ASD meltdowns can be exhausting. Prevention is better than the cure in many scenarios, which is especially true when discussing meltdowns. As a parent of a child on the spectrum, you should endeavor to form strategies that prevent them from happening as opposed to responding to them.

A crucial place to start is to identify meltdown triggers for your child, which may or may not be easy as children develop and grow; their stressors may change. Being observant and responsive is key to grasping your child's likes and dislikes. As mentioned, many HFA children can be sensitive to loud noises and bright lights, which can be unavoidable for many public places. Yet as a parent, you need to be prepared. For example, if your child isn't a fan of loud noises, but you are in an area with loud music, carry noise-canceling headphones, and be prepared to take them away if necessary. Sometimes, you might have to improvise if you can't prevent one of the meltdown triggers. For instance, you and your child are going to a brightly lit place; then be prepared with shades to protect their eyes. Examples such as this are items you can easily have handy in your sensory toolkit.

It is not possible to avoid meltdowns all the time, but there are ways you can prepare your child by:

- If there is going to be a routine change, prepare your child in advance for it and let them know so they have time to prepare.
- Show empathy and show your child that you recognize their thoughts and feelings.
- Always have their sensory toolkit to hand to divert your child's attention when you notice an oncoming meltdown.

- Teach your child how to communicate their feelings when upset (This will come with perseverance from you).

- If something in your child's daily routine is not possible, make available some other alternative or something similar that will give your child a sense of control.

- Ensuring physical concerns are not possible, such as hunger, thirst, sickness, or sleep deprivation.

- Observe and know your child, so you can try to notice an oncoming meltdown before it happens.

- Take note of the situation surrounding the previous meltdown and adjust your routine and strategy to prevent another one.

How to handle your HFA Child during a very loud, very public meltdown

Watching your child go through a meltdown is unpleasant and often exasperating. Seeing the tears and hearing the screams can be painful, and all you want to do is to make it stop.

Having a meltdown at home means you can simply walk out of the room and let your child calm down. You also don't have any external audience to witness what's happening, making the situation more manageable. There more than likely will come a time (if it hasn't happened already) when your child has a meltdown in public, with strangers as an audience.

Below are some tips you can use to help your child during a public meltdown:

Be empathetic

This simply means listening and acknowledging their feelings without making any judgment. Everyone needs to express their emotions in one way or another because we are all humans, and sometimes our feelings overwhelm us. Your job as a parent is to empathize with your child and show you care, but most importantly, you are there for them. Phrases mentioned previously in this chapter are great to comfort your child. Make sure you are extra reassuring with your words to alleviate the additional stressors bystanders may cause.

Make them feel safe and loved

It is normal for your child to get lost in what they are feeling and not hear you. Be sure to stay close to them in these public situations. Let them see you are there. It is often difficult to get through to your child when they are in the throes of a meltdown. Your presence alone will provide comfort. If you cannot get through to them when speaking to them, show that they are safe and loved by being at their side; if your child allows it, stroke them or provide light touch to ease and soothe their discomfort. Ensure not to make your child feel like they are bothering you when they are having a hard time; your message in such a time should be one of love and warmth.

Eliminate punishments

As mentioned earlier, consequences are different from punishments. Punishment can only make your child feel fearful and ashamed. Your child has no control over when the next meltdown will come, so there is no need to punish them for something totally out of their control. Give your child the freedom to express themselves in whatever they choose, unless they are causing harm to themselves or others. Let your child know that what they are going through is normal and that they won't be punished in any way.

Focus on your child, not staring at bystanders

A child going through a meltdown can be loud and overt. Strangers and bystanders will stand and watch, unknowing of their condition or disapproving of their behavior. My son's first public meltdown made me feel like I was a bad parent because I couldn't prevent the meltdown from happening, and I felt as though I were being judged. This is common for parents and often a reason why parents avoid taking their children to the supermarket or grocery store.

Forget about other people, forget about their judgmental stares and ignore all those inner fears that tell you, you are a failure as a parent. Only think about the person who needs your help, your child, because your child is the only person that matters, not the opinion of others.

Bring out your sensory toolkit

Always make sure you have a few sensory tools that can calm your child whenever they are overwhelmed. Depending on your child's sensory needs, you may need to carry noise cancellation headphones, fidget tools, or perhaps a video game. Try not to force a sensory tool on your child when they are going through a meltdown. Allow them to pick it for themselves or gently alert your child that the sensory tool is available.

———

Dealing with tantrums and meltdowns is not an easy task for any parent or carer. The first step in helping your child is identifying what they are going through. Is it a meltdown or a tantrum? Once you do, you can begin the process of helping your child through them. Always remember to maintain a clear mind and not act on your first emotion. There is no way you can help your child without first acknowledging their emotions and feelings. This is usually the first step towards calming an already tricky situation.

If you are dealing with a tantrum, be sure to remember that consequences are not there to punish your child but rather to teach them that there is a better way to behave. Explaining to your child why bad behaviors are bad is necessary to teach them that behaving in such a way is unacceptable and will only bring negative consequences. Ensure to be empathic when explaining and be explicit when detailing the importance of good behaviors.

On the other hand, if you are faced with a meltdown, the most imperative strategy to teach your child to cope better and help them during a meltdown is by focusing on the cause of the problem. Ask questions. Why is this happening? Why are they reacting like this today? Why are they stimming so much? Enforcing such analysis and investigation into the source of the problem is the answer to making your life easier and your child's life happier. Endeavor to ask the why questions, and only that way can you alleviate stressors and reduce meltdowns.

Utilizing these evaluation skills underpins the values of positive parenting. Do not be ashamed if you struggle when managing those difficult times, as it took me years to grasp. Many HFA parents would agree that you are doing a good job as long as you are using the steps to prevent meltdowns and limit tantrums. Keep doing what you are doing!

7

THE FUNDAMENTALS OF BUILDING FRIENDSHIPS

As adults, we know how friends can make our lives lighter, brighter, and happier. We understand the need for forging relationships that allow us to be true to ourselves. As adults, we may have found our best friends already, and as parents, we want our children to experience the same. However, while the majority of children may find that normal and easy, others experience building friendships differently. This is especially true for our children that have high-functioning autism.

I can still remember how difficult this phase was for my son. I was clueless. But now, looking back, I understand that anxiety will always linger with us parents, worrying if our children can ever make friends with children of their own age. Making friends alone in any environment can be hard, yet making friends with limited social skills like many HFA children makes the process even more challenging for them and us parents. Attending school and interacting with neuro-typical children who you fear will see your child as different from them seems like a frightening thought, right? More often than not, it is with these encounters that they figure out they are different. Despite the apparent challenge, you must acknowledge the key to helping them on their journey lies in your patience, encouragement, and understanding.

My son struggled with making friends practically throughout elementary school, from grade 1 to grade 5, because I didn't know then what I know now. Speaking from experience as a parent, you have to be affirmative in your beliefs. Making friends for our children is an absolute possibility! We must believe it ourselves; else, we will be consumed by our anxiety and doubts. Often, what limits us is our own thoughts, which we will eliminate for our children's sake.

There is an abundance of things that we can teach our children with high-functioning autism, to foster healthy relationships with their peers. Your child may struggle with social interaction, they may lack emotional recognition, and they certainly may have an inability to express themselves properly; however, with the right tools, your child can flourish. So, here are some ways to help your child establish friendships with other children of their age. I have tested these myself, and I can guarantee their usefulness. These tips will give you the confidence to instigate and enrich your child's friendships. Soon enough, you'll be able to further develop these strategies that are specifically tailored for your child's individual needs and preferences.

Building Interests

You can start by encouraging them to find and build their interests. Individual interests give us a feeling and sense of identity, especially on things we choose for our own. The same applies to our HFA children. Interests build confidence within them, making them feel like they belong to a particular group.

Our children often have very focused interests, which can boost learning opportunities and improve communication. However, it is not always helpful when forging new friendships. For this reason, we must help them pick an interest that would develop their confidence and benefit them in the long run. It is best to lead them to activities that will hone their skills and abilities while also allowing them to join a group with children with similar interests. For example, if your child had a creative side, you might consider buying them a paint set, leading to them joining an art club with other children of the same age. Try buying your child something that enables a new skill, and 'build on it,' do not simply buy a football, cards, drawing kit, or whatever it is you think your child could thrive in; you must nurture their interest and be involved in their development. If they are painting, try painting with them, or discuss their likes and dislikes about their painting. Having involvement like this deepens their interests, builds confidence, and boosts their self-esteem (two key elements for making friends!).

Parents as Role Models

Acting as our children's role models is another way to help them develop their social skills. As their most trusted teacher, it will be best for your child to learn these valuable lessons directly from you. As we know, HFA children have difficulty interacting with others, although as parents, you can show them how you interact with your friends, to model the correct behaviors. Children, especially at a very young age, tend to copy and adopt the personalities they observe around them, so showing them how to build and maintain a good friendship is a pivotal starting point.

In this Digital Age, it is also worth noting how 'digital' friends differ from our real-life companions. Yes, I know that we can build good friendships in both worlds, but if we wish to develop our children's social skills, we should show them real-life examples. Making friends in real life is always better than meeting friends through the web. However, your child may disagree, especially in their preteens, when their phone becomes one of the most essential factors in their life, sometimes more than you!

Online platforms can be great for connecting with other children on the spectrum and often making 'friends' worldwide. Yet, if your child first learns to befriend others in the social network, it may be challenging to physically encourage them to connect outside the web. Therefore, I ask you to tread with caution when allowing your child to use social networks. Undoubtedly, they will use it, and if this is the case, ensure you have strong firewalls and parent locks in place.

The Importance of Expression

It is essential to teach your HFA child the right way to communicate with peers in a non-verbal manner. Eye contact is important when communicating with strangers and new friends. Though it may be a little unsettling for your child, you must teach them the right amount of eye contact and its importance so that it wouldn't be a peculiar and unnatural feat for them. This is especially important when they are speaking to teachers and staff at school.

Enlighten them on how they can express their feelings through eye contact, body language, facial expression, and tone of voice. My son struggled with eye contact when talking with people he didn't know. We taught him to concentrate on the bridge of their nose or a spot on the wall above the speaker's head to avoid fleeting eye contact. Learning nonverbal communication such as this can improve their social interaction skills and help them express their feelings in front of others.

Setting-up a Playdate

Quality over quantity plays a huge role in making friends. Quality relationships elicit a connection that is based on trust and respect, although this level of connection cannot be shared with everyone. As adults, we have the same social standards, we do not expect to be friends with everyone, yet we endeavor to be respectful and polite to our colleagues. It is essential to focus on quality friends that allow your child to be themselves and have fun!

Having at least one trusted friend is a good start. A single friend who shares the same interests as them, such as painting, writing, or playing outside, will help nurture them both.

Playdates help establish a deeper and more meaningful connection between your child and another, a one-on-one get-together that they don't usually form during playgroups or large group settings such as school. When looking for the right activities to go with, always keep in mind your child's personality. Do they love staying indoors? Are they the cooperative type? Do they prefer being active or watching?

Preparing in advance for your child's playdate will help you boost your child's confidence in any given activity and can reduce worries and anxieties both for you and your child as well. Map out the activities you need to include and practice some role-playing, if required, to set a calm ambiance between your child and the child they are meeting. You can cast as your child's new friend and teach them some dialogues that will help steer the conversation seamlessly. This will deter them from getting lost with words. Practicing manners is particularly pertinent, for example, "Can I play with that toy now, please." This not only includes please but also a modal verb. Prompting your child to use modal verbs, "Can I," "May I,' will not only give your child better interaction with friends but also good communication skills when they are in more formal settings such as school.

An important factor to consider is the environment and ambiance of the playdate. An atmosphere that they are not too familiar with, such as playdates, may cause an initial negative reaction or response, but such situations are typical and should be handled with utmost patience. For this reason, you should start with shorter playdates, an hour or an hour and a half, especially if your child is a preschooler. Children in this age bracket often have a shorter attention span and can become distracted or distressed more easily. Gradually lengthen each playdate by minutes and then hours. For children in an older bracket (between 5-10), a good starting point is limiting the playdate to three hours.

To aid the playdate running smoothly, set out toys/games/arts and crafts that will be used, this way, the children can transition from one activity to the next with ease. Most children have various attachment levels to their toys, so choosing the toys that your child would want to play with someone else is crucial in planning a one-on-one get-together. As mentioned earlier, it is critical to keep in mind what interests and personalities your child possesses, so you can match your child with playmates who share the same interests and personalities as theirs.

Moreover, you should also understand that children have different types of play. It is common to urge children to play more enthusiastically or more united when watching them play; however, you should give them the freedom to play as they desire unless they are disrespectful to one another. I encouraged my son to play more attentively with his first-ever playmate as they were quietly sitting side-by-side, which is also called 'parallel play,' but I was wrong to do so, as this is still a form of play. Sitting quietly within each other's company can benefit them both.

Children can also be territorial. When one child hosts the playdate at their home, the host often tends to feel dominant over the other, which could cause tension throughout an activity. When planning playdates for your HFA child, choosing neutral places, such as private rooms, daycare, art rooms, etc., are better. This way, they are more likely to be respectful of one another. If the situation requires you to have the get-together in your child's friends' home, then you should make them understand the ground rules in entering someone else's house. An example would be refraining your child from touching or using things inside the house without the playdate's parent's permission. Aside from teaching your child to behave during playdates, you are simultaneously training them for the proper behavior of guests.

Other than the planning side of things, allowing post playdate time to unwind is important. To avoid my son from becoming overwhelmed or over-excited (especially if it is close to bedtime!), I would always allow a few hours after each playdate for him to decompress. I make sure he gets the alone time he needs, a quiet place for himself to find calm and wind down, which I cannot recommend enough for your HFA child.

Patience is the Key

As parents of a HFA child, we face different challenges every day. Just when you start to feel like you have hit a home run, then comes another puzzle for you to solve. So, it is only natural for us to feel drained by the end of the day. Many of you can relate to how these challenges are worsened by our children's battles against anxiety disorder.

Anxiety disorder is a common yet serious problem amongst children with HFA, which can lead to one or more disorders such as panic disorders and phobias. Anxiety can be a hugely inhibiting factor for our children trying to make friends. As a parent, you need to be not just understanding but empathetic. It is common to compare their childhood to your own, simple statement such as 'I had lots of friends at his/her age.' I said this to myself. The bottom line is, many parents, including myself, have gone through this experience before. There will always be concerns and worries that will linger in our thoughts, but these shouldn't limit what we do to help them forge friendships. After all, friends brighten our lives and make our days more exciting; making friends is an essential part of growing up.

———

Friendships will form and grow if you nurture the skills required and be positive about the process. These skills are essential life skills that will improve all of their relationships which is particularly important when our youngsters start school.

8

LITTLE KNOWN TRUTHS WHEN
PREPARING FOR SCHOOL

"Should we take our child to a traditional school or a special one?" That's one question every parent with a HFA child has. It is difficult to answer in a single sentence, but this chapter will help you know what you should do in this regard. We will discuss the issuance for HFA children in education, choosing the right school, weighing up your options with the pros and cons.

You will agree that finding the right school for any child is not easy, and when you are dealing with a HFA child with varying needs, it can make the process even more difficult. Thankfully, the law provides that every child should be educated and taught by teachers experienced in handling children with HFA.

. . .

Depending on your child's condition, you will have to decide if a mainstream, traditional school or a special needs school is suitable for your child. The latter, while specialized, often lack the opportunity to train children with the necessary social skills. The vast majority of parents prefer their HFA children to go to mainstream schools.

To choose the right school, you will have to visit the school and talk with the teachers and inclusion manager or SENCO, which stands for Special Educational Needs Coordinator. Organizing a meeting to discuss your child's needs and the school's facilities is essential for making your decision on the school easier. You will see, first hand, if the school has experience dealing with HFA children and if they have proven measures in place to help your child.

When there, ensure to ask as many questions that will help justify your decision. It can be overwhelming, especially if you are unfamiliar with the school system concerning HFA. A question that is a good starting place is whether they have in-house therapists and specialists.

A few other great questions:

- If the teacher has experience with autistic children

- How many students are in each class
- Can the school support your child's Individualized Educational Program (IEP)
- How the school determines that your child is learning (progress)
- Is there sufficient teaching support in your child's class, and a host of other questions.

Younger children with high functioning autism benefit from smaller classes in their early education because they often need extra attention and support to grasp school routines, a near-impossible task in a large class.

Your main task here is to find a school interested in catering to your child's unique needs while learning essential social skills from others. Let's find out how to pick the right one!

How to Choose The Right School

Taking your HFA child to a mainstream public school is not an issue. Many children with autism go to mainstream primary schools. The good thing is that your child will be exposed to social skills and interactions that will help prepare them for life's encounters.

The primary reason when selecting a mainstream

school is that the law is on your side. There are educational standards and policies that determine how schools must render help to children with disabilities, including autism. While the policy or law can differ from state to state, you can expect that the school will cooperate with you to achieve the best education for your child.

There are some mainstream schools with special units, and if you have this option in your vicinity, you are in luck. This means that your child will have access to both mainstream classes together with the support of a special class.

In the special class, often a smaller one, the specialist will take time to give each child the attention they need to grasp the topics being taught. This can often be conducted by an OT or SLT who has a tailored program for your child. To get this right, the school will need to have full details about your child's condition, which will come from you as the parent and assessments conducted by the school to ensure they will be comfortable in their classroom setting. Be sure to have open communication with the SENCO to elicit your child's best teaching and learning.

Another option is to take your child to a special school. They are schools that provide special education needs for children that need them. These particular schools have different teaching methods, so you will have to be sure that the one you choose is right for your child. Two of the most commonly utilized methods in special schools to teach children with HFA are Applied Behavior Analysis (ABA) and DIR/ Floortime.

Another option you have is private or independent schools. As the name infers, they are independent of state education authorities. Still, they follow all critical and relevant laws on education rights, discrimination, and disability. While being private schools, they can be special or mainstream.

The final option parents with HFA children can turn to is homeschooling. Different reasons why parents resort to this include, but not limited to, distance to preferred school, religious values, the child's particular needs, among others.

Choosing this option means that you will have to be fully aware of your state's education department's requirements in this regard and follow them without fail. One of the main downsides to homeschooling, however, is the cost.

Whatever option you choose, what is essential is that the school has what you want for your child. Ask questions, what are your child's needs? Does the school have resources to meet those needs? Then, ensure you start looking early enough for prospective schools as this will give you time to prepare for starting school.

. . .

Mainstream school

Public schools are full of children with different needs and backgrounds. It is also free, which means that your high-functioning autistic child may well get all the education and social skills they need. Other times, the child may struggle to find their place in the setting.

You may ask, is public school ideal for my child, or should I look to other options? The answer depends on a few things, such as what you want for your child, the school, your budget, and your child's needs.

Now, let's look at the pros and cons of having your HFA child in a public school.

Pros

- The first thing, of course, is that public school is free. According to the Individuals with Disabilities Education Act (IDEA), your child is eligible for a Free and Appropriate Public Education (FAPE) in the Least Restrictive Environment (LRE). This is simply saying that the school is expected to provide the appropriate support to ensure that your child succeeds. For this to happen, your child must have an Individualized Educational Plan (IEP). This will entail the goals and your expectations for your child.

- If you were to ever feel that the progress you expect wasn't being achieved, you could call a meeting with all stakeholders and discuss you and your child's next steps to improve on learning goals.

- Public school is excellent and one of the fastest ways for your child to gain social skills, so if they can thrive in the setting, the rewards are great. Without a doubt, social skills development is a significant challenge for HFA children. With the way public schools are structured, you may have little to worry about when developing your child's social skills – of course, that depends on whether your child can cope in the setting.

Cons

- One of the downsides of enrolling your child in a public school is that administrators may claim to be unable to provide the utmost care for your child due to administrative and budgetary constraints.

- You may also discover that your district does not provide your preferred program. Your district may only have an Applied Behavioral Analysis (ABA) program in place for their HFA students. However, you prefer developmental therapies – or vice versa. In that situation, what do you do?

- Some districts also create autism classrooms with sensory integration facilities, where they conduct their learning. However, that might not be the best for your child. After all, you have chosen a mainstream school as you want your child to learn in a typical mainstream classroom.

- It is also not uncommon to have other children bully HFA children because they tend to behave, talk and move differently from their peers. Since bullying tends to happen in public schools, it may not be the best option for your high-functioning autistic child, especially if they have accompanying sensory challenges.

- Spending the day in a loud, bright, or too crowded environment can be a severe challenge for children with sensory challenges. Unfortunately, these are some things you can expect in a public school, and oftentimes, it is a situation beyond the control of the school.

Special schools

Special schools differ from mainstream or regular schools in that they take deliberate steps to cater to students with educational challenges. When children or students have unique needs, special schools will provide the right programs, professionals, and resources to support the children.

The main goal of special schools is to provide children with age-appropriate educational resources and teach them in a format that cares and considers the children's conditions. They often employ a wide range of approaches to teach children, which we will discuss later in this chapter.

Having understood what this type of school can offer, let's see the benefits and disadvantages your child can experience in one.

. . .

Pros

- The first, and arguably the most important benefit of special schools is the necessary support they provide. Your HFA child can be offered accommodation, individualized classes, or private tutoring with specific learning aids depending on the particular school. You will not find the same level of detailed and personalized care in a mainstream school.

- Another benefit of a special school is the presence of qualified and specially trained teachers. Special schools take time to look for teachers who understand the needs of the unique children in their care and have the necessary skills to teach using manipulatives and sensory tools to promote learning.

- The size of classes in a special school are usually half the size of a mainstream school, meaning more attention and time from teaching staff.

- Your child may also be exposed to differentiated instructions to meet their learning needs. When planning to enroll your child in a special school, you and your child will be required to go through a rigorous process that helps the school understand your child's unique needs. This would include filling out questionnaires, meeting the school counselor and other health specialists the school employs. With a smaller student load, teachers and aides are able to tailor plans with specific targets to meet social and educational goals.

- Special schools often provide excellent resources and services in-house on a day-to-day basis. These can include tutoring programs, physical and occupational therapy, learning aids, academic and psychological counseling, and speech-language therapy.

- Children have the opportunity to meet peers with similar challenges and can learn to interact with others and develop social skills in an autism-friendly environment.

- Many special schools also provide education up until 18 years old and intertwine life classes into learning which helps your child transition into adulthood.

Cons

- The lack of integration jumps out first. Many parents of children with high functioning autism do not like that their children are denied the opportunity to interact with peers without special needs. They argue that their children are not exposed to a wide range of influences, which is a solid point. Society is already unfair on children with special needs; when they go to special schools, the stigma or negative connotation is further reinforced.

- Cost is another critical factor when considering a school for your child. In general, the fees to attend a special school are considerable. However, you are paying for the staff, facilities, and often extensive space the school has. It can easily be justified to spend the money; however, many families, unfortunately, cannot afford it.

- It is also not uncommon to find out that children with HFA find it difficult to relate with other children in their class or at school as the children attending may have more severe symptoms that inhibit interaction, which could affect their social growth.

- Another problem that can arise with special education is the possibility of the school lowering standards or expectations. A core teaching standard is to set high expectations; therefore, children have something to strive for and achieve. Suppose your child is attending a school with low or little expectations. In that case, the chances of progress and growth are slim and decrease the likelihood of them transitioning into higher education and societal roles later in life.

- Transitioning from a special school into another setting can be challenging to adjust academically with different class sizes and children's emotional and social effects.

Homeschooling

Many parents of HFA children are opting for home-schooling, and for good reasons. However, before you opt for this option, there are important factors you must consider.

It is essential to understand what your state laws outline regarding homeschooling; for example, some states require parents to have a certain level of education. It would help if you also had the support of your partner. Not having a united front can affect homeschooling in the long run.

Homeschooling isn't cheap. When you decide to homeschool your child, that might mean you are choosing to limit your income potential. So, can you afford it?

Aside from all that, like any other school setting, self-regulation can be an issue, and you must know how to handle it. When your child loses their temper for whatever reason, you would want to have a quiet place for them to de escalate and know how to deal with their misbehavior.

Enough words; let's look into what you tend to gain from homeschooling your HFA child and what the demerits might be.

Pros

- A calmer environment that reduces sensory stimuli is a good reason to consider homeschooling your child. One reason to dodge mainstream schools or even special schools is the sensory stimuli they can cause for your HFA child. Thankfully, homeschooling lets you take care of that.

- Many HFA children get anxious in a large class, and often the larger the class, the higher the anxiety. When homeschooling, anxiety is often eradicated.

- Taking note of medical challenges such as food allergies or intolerances can be difficult if your child is in school and you are about your daily activities. However, in a homeschooling setting, you are able to monitor what they eat and see any reactions quickly, if any. After all, when people are comfortable, they tend to learn better.

- Homeschooling also gives your child the opportunity to practice the skills they need with less pressure. Many teachers don't realize what it takes a child with HFA to accomplish even the most basic task, but you do—having you as their teacher enables rich and thorough learning as you know what your child needs to work on.

- While homeschooling, there is the advantage of being in your home environment. It provides an opportunity to teach your child life skills, such as cooking, cleaning, or gardening, which is not generally accessible in school settings. This is especially poignant if your child is older and struggling to look after themselves. My son was not a fan of washing himself when he was 9, which many boys around that age struggle with. Homeschooling can give you time and the environment to address more personal learning.

- Homeschooling drastically reduces bullying and peer pressure. Bullying can happen anywhere, not just at school. However, homeschooling helps to reduce the chances of this happening.

- One of the beauties of homeschooling is that it allows you to work on your child's weaknesses at their own pace. Is the child behind on math or reading? Do you need to spend extra time on phonics today or recap on subtraction? Homeschooling gives you the flexibility to address misconceptions effectively. Working at the child's pace will improve their strengths and build their confidence and self-esteem.

- Homeschooling also gives you the freedom to incorporate activities that won't work in a typical classroom with other children. Homeschooling lets you teach to your child's learning style and interests. Perhaps your child is a kinesthetic learner and enjoys learning by doing. Therefore you could use an entire box of lego bricks to illustrate addition in math or historical events.

- Because this is a school at home, your child doesn't have to sit at a desk all day. You could take a lesson in your backyard or work on the floor or under a pile of blankets – as long as your child is learning, you have that freedom.

- This next pro might sound counterproductive, but it is as valid as the others we have discussed. Homeschooling offers your child more success in social situations. Your child can learn a new social skill with you at home and then practice with their siblings or the neighbor, and you can monitor.

Cons

- Homeschooling can be tedious and challenging work; if you are not prepared for it in every way possible, it will overwhelm you very quickly.

- The first thing you might realize is that you aren't in the best position to teach your child because you haven't had teacher training. For this reason, you would have to take time to study subjects you aren't familiar with and grasp the curriculum targets based on your child's age.
- Your child might have some developmental problems in a homeschool setting because they cannot learn from their peers and associate with them.
- Dealing with unruly tantrums and misbehavior is something you will have to get good at.
- As mentioned earlier, homeschooling isn't cheap. You have to consider the cost of purchasing textbooks and teaching materials – but that's not all. The opportunity cost of not bringing home your income for the family is another reason most parents don't consider homeschooling. Homeschooling is a full-time job.

Preparing your child for school

Whichever schooling option you decide for your child, getting them prepared for school is another difficult task you must not handle with levity. For any child, transitioning to school can be challenging, but with a HFA child, further support is often required.

The reason being that most HFA children fail to develop the social and language skills that other children have, so they find it difficult to adapt to the new environment and routine. All hope is not lost though, as there are proven strategies in place that you can take. So, let's find out.

Helping your child visualize social stories will help them as you count down to the first day at school. To do this, you could write your own social story with pictures and names of your child's school and teachers. Read through and act out scenarios with your child to prepare them for the different social etiquettes required.

Make arrangements to meet your child's teacher and the school staff before school starts with your child to be familiar with the class setting and environment. This will help reduce anxiety. While meeting them, you should also have a school tour, with clear guidance on where the SENCO or guidance counselors office is to provide security and a sense of welcoming for your child, especially if they are in their first year at school. Try to take pictures and videos of the school to show your child before school starts to remind them of their environment and give a sense of comfort as starting school for any child is a nerve-wracking experience.

If your child will be riding a bus to school, meeting the bus driver to discuss your child's challenges is important. It would help if you also went to the bus stop with your child before school starts and on the first few days. Let your child know where to stay to wait for the bus.

In my family's case, we considered homeschooling, but it wasn't financially feasible. We loved the idea, but with a child with HFA, another with ADHD, and the youngest dyslexic, homeschooling would have been a challenge far too great!

What is important is that your child isn't anxious about starting any school. Get them excited about the new experience that awaits them and be there every step of the way.

————

Deciding the right school for your highly functioning autistic child is no easy task. You have three options to choose from, and while each has its advantages, the disadvantages cannot be neglected.

. . .

My advice to parents is this; choose the option that is best for your child. And to do that, you have to understand your child's needs completely. Don't assume you do; if you have sought after therapy and use their strengths to their advantage, you will know what is best for your child. Do not be afraid to look around schools and speak to staff. The ultimate advice is to trust your gut. You will know if a school is a right fit for your child.

9

SUPPORT SIBLINGS IN THESE 5 SIMPLE STEPS

A t this point, I must congratulate you. You have come so far on your journey, and to have read up until this point shows you are committed to improving your family's life for the better. Being a parent with an autistic child can bring many challenges and obstacles you will need to jump over. The sleepless nights, the uncomfortable last-minute decisions, and the several sacrifices you make to ensure your HFA child is ok are all intertwined into your life, which is hard on you as a parent and your family at large.

You will agree that we have been focusing on your HFA child and you from the beginning of this book. We have discussed what your responsibilities are to them and how to handle their diagnosis. We have also discussed how to use your child's interests to help them thrive and prepare them for school. In this chapter, however, we will address the importance of siblings. Yes, this book is about you and your HFA child, but you will agree that their siblings play a significant role in their development, and the better the bond, the easier parenting can be.

I mentioned bonding because unless you take time to explain to your neurotypical children the condition your HFA child has, sibling bonding can be jaded and unhealthy. Take it from someone who knows; it isn't easy to give equal time to your children as a parent. Of course, you can try, but it is much more challenging with a HFA child, if not impossible. It is very common for siblings to get lonely and frustrated because they feel you give more attention to their HFA sibling. So what then should you do? That is precisely what we will be discussing in this chapter.

There are five simple steps to be discussed, which in any family is essential to ensure that siblings are given the necessary support, and good family culture is cultivated. We will address your role to all your children and how to improve the relationship the sibling(s) have within the family.

At the end of this chapter, you will be renewed and encouraged to take the proper steps in your family and help your children support each other with tender loving care.

The Importance of Sibling Relationship

Sibling relationships in any family are special, unique, and important. Undoubtedly, brothers and sisters play essential roles and influence each other in ways more than they can comprehend. Your children's first social network is their siblings, and this relationship forms the basis of their potential relationships with friends.

Siblings are, first of all, playmates. Other roles like friend, teacher, companion, confidant, and role model can spring up as they grow. When this relationship is affected by high functioning autism, the opportunities to interact or bond may be restricted.

Typically, living with a sibling can be rewarding, instructive, confusing, and even stressful to children. Still, what I've also found out is that children typically want to show love, support, and empathy to their HFA siblings – a relief to you. However, for this to happen, a few factors must be in place. Some of these include the family's lifestyle and resources, the age difference between the children in the family, the severity of the disorder, and the coping mechanisms that exist with the family.

Each child's reaction to being a sibling of a HFA child will be different and very often is dynamic. It can change as the child understands the situation and advances in age. For instance, preschool-aged siblings might be confused, anxious, and angry about a HFA child. The younger the neurotypical child is, the more difficult it is to understand why their siblings are not exactly like them.

The importance of sibling relationships is crucial when your children are young. Your children have to bond, and this bonding is even more critical when you have a high-functioning autistic child. Ensuring your children have a sincere bond will not only aid social development in your HFA child but will increase learning opportunities for both children.

My point is this; you cannot overemphasize the importance of sibling relationships. A cordial sibling relationship means that you can care for all your children with fewer issues or wonder if the HFA child's siblings are feeling left out.

You will also have peace of mind and receive help now and then from your family members. Achieving a cordial relationship among your children rests on how you treat or support your neurotypical child or the sibling of the HFA child.

We will discuss the five steps I use to support these siblings but before then, let's quickly look into three warnings that you must be mindful of when assessing sibling relationships.

Three Warnings You Must Take Onboard

1. All siblings will fight or argue

This is one of the most profound truths about siblings. People argue, and this includes siblings who love each other deeply. You might find your children fighting for whatever reason, and you will do yourself more harm than good if you think the fighting is related to the HFA condition. It might, but it often isn't.

The point here is that your children will fight or argue, and you should try and settle it as amicably as possible. Think about it, you and your siblings probably fought while growing up over trivial things like toys and games. The same applies to your children.

2. Seize learning moments for both HFA child and sibling

More often than not, your HFA child and their siblings will teach each other. When you see this happen, and it might often happen if they bond well, seize the moment. Don't intervene unless you deem it necessary, as these learning moments are natural and pivotal to sibling connection. Let them enjoy each other's company and only guide when needed.

3. Don't compare your children. Ever.

I can't find a better way to say this. It is as simple as that – don't ever compare your children. Each of them is unique in their own way, so appreciate them every opportunity you get. Don't start thinking, 'If only Jane could get things right the way Mark does....'

No, don't ever find yourself in a position where you begin to compare your children. To take a step further, don't compare your children with other people's children. Maybe you see another high-functioning autistic child, and you feel they are doing better than your child; chances are you are wrong.

Your child is doing just fine. The problem is the moment you start comparing; you will begin to lose your joy, you will be frustrated easily and get tired altogether. So, I cannot stress enough, never compare your children. Ever.

5 Ways to Support Your HFA Child's Siblings

We have discussed the cordial relationship between your children. It is essential to discuss how you can support your neurotypical child to form an inclusive family unit and avoid feeling left out or having resentment towards you.

1. Communication

The first thing you should do is have an open, honest conversation with their sibling about HFA. You could watch a film, online videos, read books, research websites, and it is also helpful to give scenarios for them to relate. Ensure to factor in plenty of time for questions. Explain in detail your HFA child's needs and why they may come second sometimes.

You must have this conversation with them no matter how unpleasant you feel about it. This might be hard to comprehend, especially for younger siblings, but you must do it nevertheless.

You will discover that the benefits of taking time to explain this condition rather than assuming they know will not only save you from a lot of headaches but, most importantly, provide understanding and clarity for the sibling. It is common to feel out of the loop as a sibling because they are simply ignorant of their family situation.

. . .

The initial conversation is critical to ensure the children have a sincere understanding, although do not be worried if you feel they are not entirely sure of high functioning autism. With an open line of communication running both ways, the sibling will have the freedom to ask questions, and as parent, you must be honest.

Having two or more siblings is challenging, although, with a HFA child, it involves more resources, more attention, more funding, and a lot more of your energy. The latter being the most significant. It is usual for parents to assume that their NT child is doing just fine. Yet, in honesty, how often do you take the time to think about how their sibling(s) feel?

Of course, you would have, but is it a consistent thing? If not, it doesn't mean you are a terrible parent. It simply means you have to start looking from the perspective of the sibling too. The sibling is dealing with a whole new world just as much as your HFA child. For instance, some rules that don't apply to their friends will apply to them, or consequences that you have for your HFA child are not as severe. Implementing open communication is crucial to explain the reasoning behind those different situations. When you imbibe this culture, your neurotypical child can tell you about their feelings towards their sibling or a particular situation, and you can discuss with them how to overcome feelings of upset or frustration.

An open communication culture will also help these siblings understand their feelings, as it is frustrating to have to come second to your sibling. The good thing is, talking about their emotions allows you to explain 'why' you have to spend extra time with your HFA child but also be empathetic to the siblings and learn to listen. Let them express themselves, and you will quickly know if you can make a simple change to accommodate their needs as well as your HFA child. Often parents feel guilty and ashamed when siblings make their feelings known. However, it is essential to listen and learn from the siblings as they often have an outlook on family dynamics you may not have seen.

2. Be Positive

Being positive in a challenging situation is probably the hardest thing to do, but there is no other alternative. You have to understand that the situation isn't happening because you deserve it or did something wrong. It's life. It happens, and you have to embrace it. The way I see it, you could take this as an opportunity to create an incredible family culture. I also think it is an opportunity to be a better person, develop, grow, move forward, and learn.

You have a HFA child with a lot of demands and a sibling(s) feeling left out. It will not be perfect all the time. You will not get it right every time, but be positive in knowing that you are doing your best and trying your hardest.

Positivity breeds positivity.

3. Create Opportunity For One-on-one Time With Siblings, And Stick To It

I wish I could say this is an easy thing to do, but that would mean I'm lying. It is not easy. Schedules and routines will become the bane of your life, and as you know, HFA children are happier when there is a routine. Planning quality time for the sibling is hard and following through with it is even harder. However, one-on-one time with the sibling is essential to their well-being. If you have visual planners in your household and have a section of the day visually blocked out for the sibling, this alone can provide comfort and reassurance, as they know they have scheduled quality time where they can be alone with you.

If that means you will have to employ resources to take care of your HFA child, it is a sacrifice necessary for the welfare and happiness of the sibling. Create time for the siblings but ensure it is one-on-one time with them. Let them feel loved, appreciated, and cared for.

4. Respite Care

Like many families with children on the spectrum, you might be feeling guilt and shame when you want to throw the towel in. When you receive help, be happy to accept it. Taking care of a child with autism can be overwhelming, and if you think you need a time out, you more than likely do. It can be costly, and there are many levels of support available from the state, although it will help the mental and emotional well-being of the sibling and you as a parent.

Please embrace help when it comes your way. The way I see it, respite care means you are spreading love, care, and responsibility to others, so you don't get overwhelmed.

5. Create Your Family Culture

The final step to supporting your neurotypical child is by creating a family culture. Although it can take time, the benefits to your family will be tremendous. Family culture helps you create a family identity, develop family rituals, find ways to love each other, and seize any opportunity to celebrate and have fun together. The basis is that you can create a mental perception about who you are as a family and what you stand for—irrespective of other families and what is deemed normal. Endeavor to make a family unit that is conscious of each other and mindful of emotions.

Encourage the siblings to look out for each other in school. It might be useful to give them responsibilities for their HFA sibling. It could be something as small as helping them pack their school bag. This will give the sibling a sense of importance and inclusion and shows a family unit and connection. However, you must be careful not to overload siblings' responsibilities, which could become a burden for them.

Another example of building family culture could be to ban raising your voices when inside the house, instead everyone has to use a squeaky mouse voice or a different type of voice you think of on different days. The most important thing is that all your family members understand why some things are the way they are in your family, which relates to open communication.

———————

I understand that caring for an HFA child is a lot of care. However, you will agree that neglecting their siblings can be a nasty side effect of your parenting. The sibling relationship is a factor in all families that should be considered with great magnitude. Spreading your time and attention is an arduous task and is not an easy one. The siblings may be suffering in silence right now. The best thing to do is to be there for them by first understanding why your family is a little different. Take time to have regular discussions with your children and remember, never compare them. Be conscious of your efforts and embrace the family unit you create.

10

HOW TO CONFRONT THOSE EVERYDAY CONFLICTS

Caring for young children is no easy task. Even the best parents on the planet struggle sometimes. Ensuring you have done task a and b alongside duties 1, 2 and 3 is a mammoth and ongoing issue for all of us parents, so again you are not alone.

As a parent of a HFA child, you would have realized that you have a somewhat different situation from other parents. I would imagine that before reading this book you probably had strategies in place for your child, although it is also probable that those methods or strategies you have been using are no longer working.

I'm here to let you know that when everything seems not to be in your favor and you are not sure of what to do with the everyday conflicts, hope abounds.

Yes, hope abounds for you, and we will be discussing in this final chapter common everyday problems parents of HFA children face and how to overcome. We will also look into one crucial factor that will help you get through your everyday life.

To begin, it is essential to discuss your organization. Many times, the level of your organization determines your HFA child's health and happiness. Your organization determines if he or she will take their medication on time, it determines if they will show up for their appointments and progress with goals and targets set by therapists and school. For this reason, it helps if you have a visual planner. That way, not only you, but your child can have access to their schedule and day to day routines. This is also useful when planning for change, as it can be visually explained and clarified and to avoid upset or confusion. Using a visual planner is great for all the family, especially if you have siblings as you can factor in one-on-one time for them, giving them the security that they need.

When dealing with everyday issues it must be mentioned that parental fatigue is a thing. Most parents of young children can experience some level of fatigue but parents with HFA children often feel exhaustion on another level. So, if you feel tired and stressed out, that feeling is valid. It is important to take enough rest as when it is due. It is not uncommon for parents of HFA children to feel overwhelmed. However, we can both agree that if you aren't prepared or are not 100 percent, your child will suffer and they will be the one who misses out or suffers in some way. Burnout is extremely common in parents with children on the spectrum. Take time to unplug from being a parent, as a break for you as mom or dad could be the answer to resetting your system and provide the energy to persevere through your everyday life. This is separate from respite care. It may be a walk alone or a 20 min nap in the afternoon, whatever it is, it is necessary. As a parent of a HFA child there is not much reprieve in your daily routine, when they are around, you are switched on all the time. The effects of taking some time for yourself will amaze you.

Being organized and taking a well-deserved break are both essential factors to helping you and your child thrive, although there will always be those everyday battles, be it big or small that parents of high functioning autistic children face.

Everyday conflicts and how to overcome them

The thing about these conflicts is that you can't avoid them but what will save you and your family is how you deal with them. Let's see how to confront these conflicts.

Self-regulation: breathing techniques

Trouble with behavior management is common among all children. Truth be told, it is not always the easiest task to calm a child with high functioning autism, but thankfully, there are simple proven techniques that you can try. Some may require some piece of equipment and others are simply what you can try with your child.

As a parent you can endeavor, but you cannot always predict or even recognize situations that may upset your child until they happen. For instance, I once taught a young girl who had a meltdown because the school reception was being painted. The smell of fresh paint made her break down. Preventing meltdowns or tantrums is not something that is easy and often can be impossible, however you can help ease situations using breathing techniques.

- **Count to ten or recite the alphabet as slowing as you can**

Since the behavior isn't because they want attention or material things, most of the time, what to do to calm them might be as simple as counting to ten or the alphabet as slow as you can, I taught a young girl who was extremely confident with the alphabet and reciting it backwards was a sufficient challenge to regulate her emotions when she was over stressed. Using this technique will help them catch their breath and regulate their heart beat. Using something like the alphabet or numbers is a familiar exercise which they may practice in school or at home which will promote familiarity and therefore de-escalate their emotional state.

- **Listen to calming music and pay attention to the different instruments**

You could also try calming songs for your child when they are going through situations of discomfort. Depending on the child, listening to classical music or their favourite song can provide familiarity and presence of mind which enables composure and tranquility.

- **List five different things you can see in the room**

Another calming technique is to together, name different things in the room. Taking advantage of their ability to think and speak whilst upset will help them focus on something different from their feelings and provide a sense of calm.

• Hold something tactile like a piece of clay or stuffed animal

This has also shown to help HFA children when they are in stressful situations. Providing something for your child to hold and either squeeze or stroke can allow positive sensory feedback which soothes and alleviates pressures from external stressors. Either a stuffed animal or a piece of clay can help, although there are a number of objects which your child may favor.

Any or the combination of these techniques will help your child calm down.

• Methods to decompress after school or a long day: embracing mindfulness

Long hours in school filled with various activities can be overwhelming for young children, both neurotypical and high functioning autistic alike. Helping your child decompress after a day at school will not only ease their nervous system but also allow your evening and bedtime routine to flow smoothly.

One sure way to do that is through practicing mindfulness. Mindfulness is simply the deliberate effort to quiet the mind and focus on the present moment without judgement. For children with HFA, most especially, studies have shown that continuous practice of mindfulness can translate into improved behavioral and cognitive responses.

Practicing mindfulness, is indeed that. Practice. Adults who have been embracing mindfulness all their lives can still struggle to achieve only a few minutes of pure mindfulness. Therefore, do not be discouraged if you try any of the below techniques and it does not work the first, second or third time. It may be an option you will not be able to try until your child is older, however mindfulness has proven to improve mental health and emotional regulation, so why not give it a try ?

Here are some **activities** you and your HFA child may appreciate:

- **Chime listening**

Chime listening is an activity where students are

asked to listen to a particular sound to practice focusing their mind and body on that individual sound. It is an effective way to maintain attention in the present moment. Here are some steps:

- Introduce your child to the chime or any other similar instrument.
- Let your child hear the chime numerous times or let them play the instrument and have them describe what they hear and notice. (Be supportive, if they are struggling to describe the sounds, guide them)
- Let your child close their eyes and listen to the vibration of the chime.
- When the chime stops, let them pay close attention to any other sounds they hear
- They can start with sounds far away such as noises from outside the room or on the street
- Slowly bring attention to sounds that are closer. It can even get as close as hearing themselves breathing or their heart beating.
- Finally, let the child share what he or she heard throughout the process.

If your child is successful with chime listening, it could be something to incorporate into their everyday after school activities and can be performed with a whole host of instruments.

• **Body scan**

Another way to practice mindfulness is to engage in a body scan. With a body scan children are empowered to feel every inch of their body and embrace stillness. This can work with children as young as 5. I taught in a special needs school and a body scan was incorporated after drama and music lessons which were generally the more active lessons. Using a body scan for only 4 minutes was enough to instill quiet and calm.

- Find a quiet place to lie down or sit comfortably with your child.
- If in a sitting position, support the head with a headrest or against a wall and make sure their feet are firmly planted.
- Let your child get comfortable and ask them to take notice of all the places their body makes contact with the floor or chair.
- Let them either close their eyes or lower their gaze, some children find it easier to focus on the ground closest to them.
- Bring attention to each part of their body.

Let them take at least one breath and notice any sensations that are present without necessarily judging or changing them. Remind them to simply notice.

- Guide them on their body scan by describing their body parts starting with their feet and then move upwards to the ankles, lower legs, upper legs, hips, chest, arms, wrists, shoulders and head.

Encourage them to feel their whole body and nothing more. There are many guided meditations you can listen to online, although if you talk them through the steps to relaxation it will not only be more personal but increase the bond you have with your child. Body scans can be used in many overwhelming situations. Once your child gets accustomed to the body scan, they can incorporate it into their daily activities and even try it when you are not there.

- **Conscious breathing**

Being mindful of your breath is a good way to soothe the nervous system, release tension, relieve anxiety, and create feelings of general wellbeing. For high functioning autistic children, you can increase breath awareness by making it tangible. Let them see, touch and feel their breath.

You could use feathers, tissues or even a piece of paper so they can see as their breath moves objects through the air. Aside from creating mindfulness, this exercise also builds eye-hand coordination, right-left brain integration, as well as fine and gross motor skills. For this to work, you and your child simply need to hold lightweight objects in your hand such as a feather, breath onto it and watch as it flies away. Do this several times. The practice may seem simple, but don't be deceived; it puts your child in the present moment, and engages them mentally and physically which underpins the essence of mindfulness. If your child is young, they will find this exercise super fun!

- **Mindful walking**

Another way to embrace mindfulness is through mindful or deliberate walking. Mindful walking helps to reduce anxiety and gives us an awareness of where our body is in space. This includes the components of the joints, muscles, and tendons that gives us a subconscious awareness of our body position at a particular point in time.

· · ·

To practice mindful walking with your child;

- Try a slow walk either indoor or outside.
- Feel the shift of your body weight, as you move, from your heel to the front of your foot.
- Take note of the texture difference as you move from one material to another. Have your child walk barefoot and feel the difference between carpet, grass, concrete or whatever you have. Ask your child about the differences and encourage them to think and feel at the same time.
- If you are limited in space, you could create a labyrinth in a spiral or figure eight shape. Then slowly walk the pattern.
- To strengthen your child's motor planning skills, you could ask them how they will feel when they walk on these different textures and at various speeds before you walk them.

There are several mindfulness practices you can take up with your child. Remember, to have fun with it, being mindful is not easy as an adult, the goal is to be aware of the present moment. If you are present for 1 minute out of 5 then you are still achieving mindfulness.

When you are mindful, you increase your ability to regulate emotions, decrease anxiety, stress, and depression. Mindfulness also helps one to focus attention, observe thoughts and feelings from an objective perspective.

Some of the other mindfulness practices include yoga, dedicated quiet time, sensory workbook, cooking activity with visual recipe, listening to classical music and a host of others.

Picky eaters

Eating or feeding is a common topic among parents of young HFA children. With high functioning autistic children, you may find out that they have eating problems and are extremely particular. When this happens, you should consider behavioural, environmental, and sensory difficulties. Let's look into these difficulties and what you can do to overcome them.

Environmental problems can also affect your child's eating and feeding. This could be characterized by selective eating and strong negative reaction to the introduction of new foods. When this occurs, you would need to examine your child's eating habits and the sensory variables. What are the types of food your child likes to eat? Where, when, how, and with whom do they eat? Successfully answering these questions will not only help you understand the type of food your child wants but also aid in introducing new types of food.

For instance, with my son, we discussed the texture of the type of food he liked and then we tried to incorporate foods with similar texture into his diet. The truth is this; it didn't always work, but we were successful with several different roasted vegetables!. Aside from food texture, your child may prefer that all their foods be at room temperature. That means food like ice cream is a no and cooked food will have to be left for a while before they can be eaten. Other times, your child may be affected by the smell of the food. So, food with an unfamiliar smell may affect their ability to eat.

Like I have mentioned, your child's eating pattern can be affected by a few things, however, you can assist them in building tolerance to new foods, and this comes with understanding your child. A solid foundation is to eat together as a family, this will encourage your child to eat. When you want them to try out different foods, be an example by eating them yourself. Another means to improve your child's eating pattern could be by limiting eating time to a reasonable amount of time, as it can be common for HFA children to take over an hour to eat their dinner. Using a timer and clear verbal timing prompts may help your child through meals.

Sleeping

Large percentage of HFA children have trouble sleeping. A year old requires about 14 hours of sleep every day while 17-year-olds need at least 8 hours of sleep. However, studies have shown that many high functioning autistic children go about their day sleep deprived. Worse, you as the parent are sleep deprived too!

If your child wakes up over and over again throughout the night, wants you to lie with them, or needs to lay in your bed to sleep, you are not alone. Trouble sleeping is incredibly common and something that should not be ignored. As mentioned in chapter 5, the strategy I had when my son was young was to play the same 5 songs before bed and use the same scripted goodnight routine every night.

Scripting, as mentioned can be frowned upon for development, although in many cases, it does not last for long. Having a scripted routine for us was the comfort he needed to self-soothe his stressors to sleep well. Do not be ashamed if you have a peculiar routine in place, as whatever routine works, is the right one for your family at that moment in time—which does not mean it can not change!

· · ·

Other things you could try include;

- Remind your child when bedtime is near. You could use an alarm clock or remind them fifteen to thirty minutes before it is time to prepare for bed. This helps them to mentally prepare and wind down.
- Help your youngster relax before bed time comes. Bath time and reading are both great for calming the senses and allowing bonding between you and your child.
- When bedtime is near, it is wise to let your child avoid the television and if you allow evening snacks, foods with caffeine like chocolate is not a good idea.

If you are struggling and nothing seems to be working, seek professional help as your child may be suffering from insomnia. If that is the case, medication supplements such as Melatonin might help. When my son was very young, we put a few drops of lavender in raw rice and allowed him to play with it before bed. The smell of lavender and sensory reception allowed him to focus consciously on the smelly rice and create a sense of calm.

. . .

Your mindset

Dealing with your mindset could as well be the first thing we should discuss in this chapter considering its importance, but you would want to save the best for the last, right?

Your mindset is perhaps the most important thing when caring for an HFA child. You have got to be affirmative. Always remind yourself that your child is unique and that you are blessed. Repeat it to yourself daily until it is a habitual act. The way you think is determined by your mindset. Seeing your situation as difficult and challenging is a primary step in the right direction. Overcoming adversity and the challenges starts with how you perceive the situation and thus deal with it. Utilising your positive mindset will enable you to not just see that your child is unique but also allow you to get to know your child.

Since HFA children often find it difficult to express themselves, take it as a responsibility to know what they want and dislike. Get to know your child as yourself. Remember, with connection comes understanding. In doing so, don't forget to make time for fun. It is possible to be swamped in all the responsibilities but what is a life without fun? Take time to just have fun and enjoy life.

You should also believe in your child's ability. Like

any other person, your HFA child wants to know that you love them and that you would support them. Of course, you do love your child, but you have to let them know. Tell them with every opportunity you have. Show them that you love and support them. Express your love to your child. In love, also learn to respect them. Respect their decisions. Of course, you would want to know why they don't want to do something, but respecting their decision will help you know your child better and help them trust you with their fears.

———

Caring for a high functioning autistic child is no easy task. Every other day you might have to deal with one issue or another. Still, you can take joy in all the everyday triumphs you will overcome and the obstacles you will learn from while taking care of your child.

It is not uncommon for HFA children to struggle with eating or have trouble sleeping. However, with you, a loving and accommodating parent by their side, they can overcome their worst fears. You are a positive parent and also one who will make a difference.

The everyday conflicts we have discussed in this chapter are things you can't, sadly, escape. The good news is that you are not alone but most importantly, there are solutions. Your answer is in first getting to know who really your child is and then using that information to care for them.

YOU ARE IN FOR AN EXCITING JOURNEY AND I HOPE YOU ENJOY IT.

CONCLUSION

As the book comes to an end, we have discussed a lot about you and your high-functioning autistic child in these ten chapters. This, then, looks like a good place to discuss the takeaways of this book.

Caring for young children is one of the most demanding jobs on the planet, and I agree with you that caring for a HFA child can be even more complicated. Thankfully, we have seen that you are more than capable of doing this job.

If you felt overwhelmed initially, I trust you are in a better place now, seeing that you are not alone and have a long list of support at your fingertips.

When my first child was diagnosed with HFA, I didn't know what to think, and I was unsure how best to care for him. However, I was happy to get the help I needed. Now, I'm doing the same for you. Take time to read this book as often as you want to, and be sure to put into practice as much content you find relevant to your child. Chief of those things to remember is that your child is unique. That could mean many things for lots of parents, but in my case, it meant that I had to be positive and pay more attention to my child. I had to listen to his actions as well as his inactions. In those times, I began to understand what he wanted and why he wanted those things.

When you begin to understand your child, that is when you can discover how to best care for them. It may seem like a simple answer for the end of this book, but putting in the time and effort to truly unpick your child's behavior and personality will help you build their character into the person you want them to become.

You will also discover, among other things, how to teach them life skills and what school to take them to. One of such life skills that may be difficult for a HFA child is making friends, and we discussed the practical steps to take, among other things, in chapter seven.

This book is indeed about you and your HFA child, but you cannot forget their siblings in all of this because they have an essential role to play in the family. Chapter nine helped us iron out how to support siblings in five simple steps, primarily having open communication.

There are always everyday problems parents deal with when their children are still young. These problems can often seem impossible! However, there are known strategies to confront these conflicts or issues. The last chapter was dedicated to this cause.

Yes, your journey as a parent may be different from your neighbor's, but you can take solace in the fact that you are not alone. You and a host of other parents who have HFA children are superheroes, and the world just got better because you didn't give up.

You will agree that all you need to go through life happy and fulfilled is a positive mindset. Perhaps the most prominent takeaway I would like you to go away with. When you are optimistic about yourself and everything around you, you can be a better person and the right parent for your child. Needless to mention that your mindset determines your realities. Will you have a positive mindset while caring and nurturing your HFA child or give up on the first hurdle? I hope you agree with me on the former. When you have a positive mindset, you automatically become a positive parent. A positive parent that wants the best and does everything in their power to help their child achieve their goals.

Now, then, is the time for action. Each time you are faced with a daunting situation, I believe you can find something to use in this book to help you. You have the tools to strive and your child to thrive. Be proud that you are taking steps to *do* better and *be* better.

I wish you all the loving success on your new journey.

If you find this book helpful and have enjoyed any of the practical strategies we have discussed, please leave a review on Amazon today.

RESOURCES

Alli, R. (2020, December). *What Are the Treatments for Autism?* WebMD. https://www.webmd.com/brain/autism/understanding-autism-treatment

A.O.T.A. (2021). *Supporting Parents of Children With Autism: The Role of Occupational Therapy.* American Occupational Therapy Associations. https://www.aota.org/About-Occupational-Therapy/Professionals/CY/Articles/Parents-Autism.aspx

ARCH National Respite Network and Resource Center (2019). *Medicaid Waivers for Respite Support.* Chapel Hill, NC: Author. Report prepared for ARCH by Kathy Mayfield-Smith, Research Associate Professor, Division of Medicaid Policy Research, Institute for Families in Society at the University of South Carolina.

Bangara, S. (2015, March 9). *Cognitive Behavioural Therapy for Anxiety Disorders in Children and Youth with High-Functioning Autism: Implementing an Evidence-Based Psychosocial Intervention.* Integrated Treatment Services. https://www.integratedtreatmentservices.co.uk/blog/cognitive-behavioural-therapy-anxiety-disorders-children-youth-high-functioning-autism-implementing-evidence-based-psychosocial-intervention/

Barloso, K. (2021, May 7). *Managing Autism Meltdowns, Tantrums and Aggression.* Autism Parenting Magazine. https://www.autismparentingmagazine.com/autism-meltdowns/

Bennie, M. (2017, March). *Bone Tired: Autism and Parental Fatigue.* Autism Awareness Center Inc. https://autismawarenesscentre.com/bone-tired-autism-and-parental-fatigue/

Brenecki, J. (2014). *10 Tips for HFA.* Talking Matters Speech Pathology and Occupational Therapy. https://www.talkingmatters.com.au/blog/10-tips-for-hfa/

C, A. (2019, April 1). *The Stages of Grieving Your Child's Autism Diagnosis.* Houston Moms. https://houston.momcollective.com/the-stages-of-grieving-your-childs-autism-diagnosis/

Child Mind Institute. (2021). *What Every Autistic*

Girl Wishes Her Parents Knew. Child Mind Institute. https://childmind.org/article/every-autistic-girl-wishes-parents-knew/

David Institute. (2021, July). *Common Gifted Parenting Challenges*. David Institute. https://www.davidsongifted.org/resource-library/

Hammer, D. (2020, July 24). *A Sense of Community – The Benefits of Joining Autism Parent Support Groups*. Shine Light. https://shine-light.org/parent-support/a-sense-of-community-the-benefits-of-joining-autism-support-groups-fayetteville-for-parents/

Hirsch, L. (2015, September). *Disciplining Your Child With Special Needs*. Kids Health from Nemours. https://kidshealth.org/en/parents/discipline-special.html

Huang, A. and Wheeler, J. (2006). INTERNATIONAL JOURNAL OF SPECIAL EDUCATION. *EFFECTIVE INTERVENTIONS FOR INDIVIDUALS WITH HIGH-FUNCTIONAL AUTISM*, 21(3).

Hutton, M. (2015). *Building High Self-Esteem in Kids on the Autism Spectrum*. My ASD Child. https://www.myaspergerschild.com/2011/04/building-high-self-esteem-in-aspergers.html

Hutton, M. (2016a). *Education & Support for Parents of Children & Teens on the Autism Spectrum*.

My ASD Child. https://www.myaspergerschild.-com/2020/04/how-cbd-gummies-can-help-with-autism.html%20),

Hutton, M. (2016b). *High-Functioning Autism and Sibling Issues.* My ASD Child. https://www.myasperg-erschild.com/2009/07/aspergers-syndrome-and-siblings.html

Hutton, M. (2016c). *"Special Interest" or Obsessive-Compulsive Disorder?* My ASD Child. https://www.myaspergerschild.com/search?q=obsessions

Hutton, M. (2019, May 2). *Reasons Behind "Impaired Social Interaction" in Aspergers and HFA Kids.* My ASD Child. https://www.myaspergerschild.-com/2013/04/reasons-behind-impaired-social.html

Interactive Autism Network. (2011, February). *SOCIAL SKILLS INTERVENTIONS: GETTING TO THE CORE OF AUTISM.* https://iancommuni-ty.org/cs/what_do_we_know/social_skills_interventions

Larkey, S. (2018). *MANAGING SCREEN TIME FOR STUDENTS WITH AUTISM.* Sue Larkey. https://suelarkey.com.au/managing-screen-time-for-students-with-autism/

Lowry, L. (2016). *3 Things You Should Know About Echolalia.* The Hanen Centere. http://www.hanen.org/Helpful-Info/Articles/3-Things-You-Should-Know-About-Echolalia.aspx

Mandell, D. and Salzer, M. (2007). US National Library of Medicine National Institutes of Health. *Who Joins Support Groups among Parents of Children with Autism?*, *10*, 111–122. https://www.ncbi.nlm.nih.gov/pmc/articles/PMC2861432/

Marcus Autism Center. (2020). *Kids with autism need friends, too.* Marcus Autism Center. https://www.marcus.org/autism-resources/autism-tips-and-resources/helping-kids-with-autism-make-friends

Marcus Autism Center. (2021). *Managing your child's screen time—7 steps that can help.* Marcus Autism Center. https://www.marcus.org/autism-resources/autism-tips-and-resources/managing-screen-time

Melinda Smith, M.A., Jeanne Segal, Ph.D., And Ted Hutman, Ph.D. (2020, November). *Helping Your Child with Autism Thrive.* Help Guide. https://www.helpguide.org/articles/autism-learning-disabilities/helping-your-child-with-autism-thrive.htm

Meyers, M. (2021, February). *How Parents Can Help Their Child With Autism Build Friendships.* We Have Kids. https://wehavekids.com/parenting/How-to-Help-Your-Child-With-Autism-Develop-Meaningful-Friendships

Milam, S. (2018, April). *When My Son With Autism Melts Down, Here's What I Do.* Healthline. https://www.healthline.com/health/autism/what-to-do-autism-meltdown#What-to-do-during-a-very-loud,-very-public-meltdown

National Respite Network And Resource Center. (2021). *A Consumer Guide for Family Caregivers.* National Respite Network and Resource Center. https://archrespite.org/consumer-information

Patel, K. (2017). *Six Simple Mindfulness Practices for Kids with Autism.* Stages Learning. https://blog.stageslearning.com/blog/six-simple-mindfulness-practices-for-kids-with-autism

Pingree, C. (2021). *The 10 Best Sensory Toys & Gifts for Children with Autism.* Carmen B. Pingree Autism Center of Learning. https://carmenbpingree.com/blog/best-sensory-toys-for-children-with-autism/

Pohlman, D. & Thienemann, M. (2016) PANDAS and PANS in School Settings: A Handbook for Educators

Raising Children. (2020). *Sensory sensitivities: autistic children and teenagers.* Raising Children.Net.Au The Australian Parenting Webiste. https://raisingchildren.net.au/autism/behaviour/understanding-behaviour/sensory-sensitivities-asd

Rudy, L. (2019). *Autism and Sensory Overload.*

Very Well Health. https://www.verywellhealth.-com/autism-and-sensory-overload-259892

Rudy, L. (2020a, September). *Educational Options for Children With Autism*. Very Well Health. https://www.verywellhealth.com/educational-options-for-children-with-autism-260393

Rudy, L. (2020b, November). *How to Calm a Child With Autism*. Very Well Health. https://www.very-wellhealth.com/how-to-calm-a-child-with-autism-4177696

Rudy, L. (2020c, December). *Sending an Autistic Child to Public School*. Very Well Health. https://www.verywellhealth.com/public-school-and-autism-education-pros-and-cons-260395

Rudy, L. (2021, June 18). *The Challenges of Living With High-Functioning Autism*. Very Well Health. https://www.verywellhealth.com/why-high-function-ing-autism-is-so-challenging-259951

SLT Kids. (2021). *High Functioning Autism*. SLT For Kids. https://sltforkids.co.uk/conditions-we-treat/high-functioning-autism/

Snyder, C. (2019, November 5). *Coping With Grief After an Autism Diagnosis*. Very Well Health. https://www.verywellhealth.com/coping-with-grief-after-an-autism-diagnosis-260273

Stevens, C. (2021). *Planning Playdates for Kids with*

Autism. Family Education. https://www.familyeducation.com/planning-playdates-kids-autism

Suni, E. (2020, July). *Melatonin and Sleep.* Sleep Foundation. https://www.sleepfoundation.org/melatonin

Trautwein, A. (2020). *Create The Best Home Environment For Your Autistic Child.* The Mom Kind. https://www.themomkind.com/create-the-best-home-environment-for-your-autistic-child/

Wheeler, M. (2018). *Mealtime and Children on the Autism Spectrum: Beyond Picky, Fussy, and Fads.* INDIANA UNIVERSITY BLOOMINGTON. https://www.iidc.indiana.edu/irca/articles/mealtime-and-children-on-the-autism-spectrum-beyond-picky-fussy-and-fads.html

Wheeler, M. (2021). *Getting Started: Introducing Your Child to His or Her Diagnosis of Autism.* INDIANA UNIVERSITY BLOOMINGTON. https://www.iidc.indiana.edu/irca/learn-about-autism/getting-started-introducing-your-child-to-his-or-her-diagnosis-of-autism.html

Wright, J. (2018, October). *Siblings of children with autism have social, emotional problems.* Spectrum. https://www.spectrumnews.org/news/siblings-children-autism-social-emotional-problems/

Made in the USA
Las Vegas, NV
18 June 2024

91217795R00115